# WINTER BIRD FEEDING

## An Alberta Guide

by Myrna Pearman

Editing Consultants - Dorothy Dickson and Sheryl Nixon
Illustrated by Gary Ross
Cover Design by Gary Ross
Foreword by Marjorie & Kerry Wood
Desktop Publishing by Myrna Pearman and Ken Larsen

Published by:
Ellis Bird Farm Ltd.
Box 2980, Lacombe, Alberta
Canada    TOC 1SO
Phone: (403) 346-2211

Second Printing, 1991


Canadian Cataloguing in Publication Data

Pearman, Myrna, 1956-
   Winter bird feeding


   Includes bibliographical references.

   ISBN 0-9694221-0-5

   1. Birds, Attracting of. 2. Birds - Alberta.
3. Birds - Food. I. Dickson, Dorothy. II Ross,
Gary, 1961-. III. Title.
QL676.5.P42 1989      639.9'78297123     C89-091624-1

## Photography Credits

Cover Photo - Gordon Johnson, Delburne

Blue Jay - Ruth Stewart, Red Deer
American Tree Sparrow - Myrna Pearman, Sylvan Lake
Mountain Chickadee - Andrius Valadka, Calgary
Evening Grosbeak - Mark A. Degner, Edmonton
American Robin - Myrna Pearman
Woodpeckers - Myrna Pearman
Boreal Chickadee - Myrna Pearman
Gray Jay - Dave Elphinstone, Calgary
Black-capped Chickadee - Murray Mackay, Ponoka
Common Redpoll - Murray Mackay
House Sparrows - Ruth Stewart
Pygmy Owl - William McNutt, Rocky Mountain House
Red Squirrel - Ruth Stewart
Nuthatches - Andrius Valadka
Clark's Nutcracker  - Cliff Wallis, Calgary

# Contents

# Acknowledgements

The production of this book would not have been possible without funding assistance from Union Carbide Canada Ltd. through its generous support of Ellis Bird Farm Ltd. The patience, encouragement and support of Ellis Bird Farm board members Ken Larsen, Fred Schutz, Dell James, Eldon Neufeld, Charlie and Winnie Ellis, Howard Fredeen, Don Young, Walter Lindley and Orest Litwin is gratefully acknowledged.

I would also like to thank the dozens of birders and feeder operators across Alberta who so freely shared with me their time, notes and observations. Special thanks goes to Kevin Van Tighem, Mike McIvor, Roy Richards, Margaret Makin, Terry Hamill, Janice Smith, Bruce McGillivray, Cleve Wershler, Dave Prescott, Bill Sharp, Michael O'Brien, Mary Reiser, Hans and Sadie Bernes, Ruth Quinn, Ray and Ardel Harris, Ruth Stewart, Aaron Collins, Charis Cooper, Laurine and William McNutt, R.L., Mairi Babey, Jack Chisholm, Harold Janecke, Jim and Lynn Newnham, Ron and Margaret Underwood, Marion Liles, George and Betty Flewwelling, Kim Fraser, Doug Meston and Robin McDonald.

I am especially indebted to those who, in addition to providing valuable information, graciously agreed to read and comment on the manuscript: Kerry and Marjorie Wood, Tom Webb, Jean and Glenn McCullough, Richard Klauke, Harold Pinel, Dave Elphinstone, Joan Susut, Joanne Susut, Mary Dawson, Dorothy Murray, Marie Pijeau, Cal and Blanche Lockhart, Murray Mackay, Corinne Tastayre, Hardy Pletz and Jane Burns.

The assistance of Parkland Colorpress and ABL Photographics staff is also acknowledged. Thank you also to Ken Larsen and John Lee for their layout advice and expertise, and to Gordon Johnson, Ruth Stewart, Murray Mackay and Dave Elphinstone for donating the use of their photographs.

To Gary Ross, whose incredible artwork graces the pages of this book, and whose creativity and talent is matched only by his patience, my thanks.

Finally, a very special thank you to my consulting editors, Dorothy Dickson and Sheryl Nixon, for their assistance, advice and red felt pens.

M.P.

# Foreword

The pleasure of seeing and hearing birds around our homes has been one of the great benefits to humankind for many generations. Long has it been a challenge to entice them to remain near our dwelling places, that we may enjoy the beauty of their plumages and thrill of their songs. The avian species of summer take to our endeavors in larger numbers, but it is in the winter months that those which stay may need our attention even more.

Myrna Pearman has undertaken a mammoth task in preparing a handbook of information and encouragement for any bird lover to follow in that service. She is not only experienced in the practical measures of providing for birds, but she has shown her love for them in her study and photography of the many species available to Alberta bird watchers.

Here the reader will find descriptions, not only of the identifiable features of birds, but of their characteristics as well, so that we may better understand the visitors to our feeders. The fine illustrations are a great help in that regard.

Those of us who have been offering wild birds food and water for many years will enjoy the comments and observations of other enthusiasts, and will find interesting new "wrinkles" to try. There is an excellent listing of nature organizations and a reading list of other fine reference material for both amateur and veteran.

Birds have amusing and entertaining characters among their throng, and whoever becomes a convert to their care and protection will have delightful hours of fulfilling companionship as a reward. We would urge any enthusiast to add "Winter Bird Feeding - An Alberta Guide" to a home bookshelf.

*Marjorie and Kerry Wood,*
*Red Deer, Alberta*

# Ellis Bird Farm Ltd.

Ellis Bird Farm Ltd. is a non-profit charitable organization dedicated to the study, preservation and enhancement of populations of cavity nesting birds, especially Mountain Bluebirds.

Initiated in 1981 by Union Carbide Canada Ltd. with the assistance of the Red Deer River Naturalists, this organization honors the name of Lacombe-area conservationists, Charles and Winnifred Ellis. The Ellises established a Mountain Bluebird nestbox trail on their farm in the mid-1950s. By 1980, when Union Carbide purchased their farm, they had earned an international reputation for having the highest nesting density of Mountain Bluebirds ever recorded on the North American continent. Ellis Bird Farm Ltd., which is administered by a volunteer board of directors, now bears the responsibility for preserving and enhancing the work pioneered by Charlie and Winnie.

In addition to managing and gathering scientific data on a nestbox trail of 560 nestboxes in the Lacombe area, the Ellis Bird Farm has initiated a number of youth and adult educational programs related to cavity nesting bird conservation and winter bird feeding.

For more information about cavity nesting birds or the Ellis Bird Farm, please write: Ellis Bird Farm Ltd., Box 2980, Lacombe, Alberta TOC 1SO. Phone (403) 346-2211.

# GETTING STARTED

Blue Jay

American Tree Sparrow

Mountain Chickadee

# GETTING STARTED

## HARDSHIPS OF AN ALBERTA WINTER

Surviving an Alberta winter, with its bitterly cold temperatures, fierce winds and deep blankets of snow, is a challenge that few bird species can meet. It is not the cold, the wind and the snow that forces so many species to depart for southern climates, however; they leave because their once abundant food sources suddenly become scarce or out of reach.

Birds that are unable to subsist on a winter menu reduced to the bare essentials of seeds, berries, buds and frozen insects must migrate. The species most affected, of course, are those whose primary summer food consists of flowering plants (which go to seed or are covered up by snow), those which eat flying or ground-dwelling insects (which freeze and die or are covered by snow) and those whose food is in or near water (which freezes). The species that can find a winter food supply (including, on occasion, American Robins, White-throated Sparrows and other "summer" birds) are able to stay here.

This is when backyard bird feeding becomes important. Feeding stations provide birds with a constant and readily available supply of food, reducing the time and energy required to search for other food sources.

Bird feeding programs aren't just good for the birds, though. People of all ages and from all walks of life are discovering that feeding birds is enjoyable and can provide opportunities to learn about and care for wildlife. It can provide hours of entertainment for senior citizens and can spark in children a lifelong interest in wildlife and conservation.

## THE BASICS

Setting up a successful winter bird feeding program is relatively simple. By following the basic guidelines suggested in this book, you will greatly increase your chances of attracting patrons to your outdoor bistros. Keep in mind that the abundance and distribution of winter bird species varies across the province, and that food preferences and feeding habits may also vary from region to region, by season and among individual birds.

While most people feed birds only during the late fall, winter and early spring months, some prefer to keep at least one or two feeding stations active year round. The latter may attract summer bird species to your backyard and may encourage resident birds, which remain in an area throughout the year, to introduce their new families to feeding stations during the summer.

There are some who fear that winter feeding programs, once initiated, must not be stopped because the birds become wholly dependent on this one food source. Stephen Kress, in his excellent book *The Audubon Society Guide to Attracting Birds*, argues that this is not usually true. He points out that birds are opportunistic and will readily eat any suitable food that they find while moving about in their relatively large winter territories. Since feeders represent only one of many food sources, they usually supplement, rather than compose the bulk of, a wild bird's diet. To a bird, a full feeder and a cone or seed-laden tree are one and the same. Likewise, a recently emptied feeder is no different from a tree just stripped of its once plentiful cones, seeds or berries.

Well-stocked feeders make life a lot easier for winter birds, however, and can actually increase their survival rates under prolonged, extremely cold, windy conditions. This is especially true for smaller birds, which lose heat quickly because of their comparatively high proportion of skin surface to body mass.

Dr. Margaret Brittingham from Pennsylvania State University recently investigated the effects of feeders on populations of chickadees. In her study area, 69% of the chickadees near feeders survived the entire winter. In the woodlands with no feeders, only 37% survived. The differences in survival rates were greatest in months when temperatures fell below -18°C (0°F) for more than five days. In warmer months, survival of both feeder and non-feeder birds was comparable. Dr. Brittingham suggests that the birds try to "sit out" cold spells by becoming lethargic and by sitting motionless with their feathers fluffed out. Hunting under these conditions would use up more energy than would be gained by eating.

The chickadees that had access to the feeders in Dr. Brittingham's study area were fatter and could obtain their food with less energy expenditure than their counterparts relying solely on wild food. She concluded that feeders do increase the survival rate of chickadees in extremely cold weather. To find out more about Dr. Brittingham's study and other topics related to winter bird feeding, join Project FeederWatch (see page 59 for more details).

On rare occasions, an individual bird may linger behind at a feeder (usually a seed feeder) when the rest of its species have followed their natural instincts and migrated south for the winter. These individuals, which are not adapted to our harsh winters, often become wholly dependent on feeder food and will usually perish if it is withheld or terminated, especially in extremely cold weather. In these situations, it is imperative that a feeding program continue uninterrupted until the bird's natural food becomes available again in the spring.

In most cases, however, the real problem with being inconsistent at topping up your feeders is that the birds will soon overlook your feeders in favor of those belonging to your more reliable neighbors!

## THE IMPORTANCE OF TREES

The presence of trees or shrubs near a feeder is absolutely essential. Trees offer both food and protective cover to most winter bird species and few, with the exception of redpolls and Snow Buntings, will venture far from the security of a wooded area. If your backyard has no trees, or has only a few small ones, chances are that your feeder will not be very popular no matter how hard you try to entice birds to it. The most effective way to attract birds and other wildlife to your backyard is to incorporate a feeding program into a landscaping plan that offers year round habitat. A backyard can be turned into a haven for birds by planting trees and shrubs that provide cover or produce fruits and berries. For more information on wildlife plantings and attracting backyard wildlife see page 63.

## LOCATION

Take a few minutes to plan the most favorable locations for your feeders before you set them out. Ideal sites are in protected areas on the south side of a house or other buildings near shrubbery. Feeders placed too close to trees may be subject to surprise attacks by hungry cats or used as landing strips by squirrels, which can jump up to 2.7 m (9 ft). A feeder placed too far from trees, on the other hand, may unduly expose your patrons to a passing hawk or shrike.

You may want to start by placing your feeders a good distance from your house, then gradually bringing them in closer for better viewing. Make sure the locations you choose will be easily accessible to both you and the birds throughout the winter.

## WHAT TO FEED?

Winter bird food is generally of three varieties: seeds, suet (including fat and bone sawdust) and gourmet treats. Keep in mind that by providing a variety of foods in different feeders placed at various locations, you will increase your chances of attracting a greater diversity of birds. You will also reduce the competition at each feeder. Large feeding areas are preferable to smaller ones, as they tend to reduce aggression and competition. It is generally best to provide only one type of seed per feeder (see page 19 for more details).

## THE QUESTION OF EXOTIC SPECIES

While it is unfair to label an individual bird or an entire species as "good" or "bad", many feeder operators go to considerable efforts to discourage the introduced House Sparrow, European Starling and Rock Dove from using their feeding stations. Many naturalists also question the merit of introducing game birds into Alberta, so, on principal, prefer not to feed Ring-necked Pheasants, Gray Partridges or Wild Turkeys. The decision on whether or not to feed exotic species is one that must be made by each individual feeder operator.

# ATTRACTING WINTER BIRDS WITH SEEDS

Evening Grosbeak

Black-capped Chickadee

Common Redpoll

# SEED FEEDING

Seed feeders are designed to attract species whose main summer diet also consists of seeds. They are usually set out in September and maintained throughout the winter until April or early May. Feeders set out in early fall often attract migrant birds attempting to build up their fat reserves for the long journey south and may also encourage resident or over-wintering species to include your backyard in their winter territories.

Year round seed feeding stations are becoming increasingly popular, as they often attract White-crowned, Savannah and other native sparrows in the spring and fall, and such summer species as American Goldfinches, Pine Siskins, Purple Finches and Rose-breasted Grosbeaks.

Except during prolonged periods of bitterly cold winter weather, don't worry about having to interrupt your seed feeding program unless, as was mentioned in the previous section, you happen to attract an individual bird that normally would have migrated south. In this case, you should make every effort to provide a constant food supply until the bird can find its own food in the spring.

You may notice that some seed-eating species, such as crossbills, grosbeaks and redpolls, are abundant at your feeders one year and absent the next. You may also notice considerable variation in population numbers from month to month. Biologists refer to these species as being "irruptive migrants", since they frequently move about in large winter territories and will often move to new areas each winter. Their presence or absence at your feeders reflects the availability of other food sources, especially spruce cones. It has nothing to do with your feeding program.

## BUYING AND STORING SEEDS

Seeds, which are less expensive if purchased in bulk, can be acquired at nature centres, feed mills and pet or livestock feed stores. Avoid supermarket or hardware store seed packages, as they usually contain filler material and less-preferred seed (see page 19 for more details).

Sunflower seeds are usually purchased in 20 kg (44 lb) or 22 kg (50 lb) bags. Keep the bag in a dry, secure location. If dampness or such uninvited diners as mice or squirrels are a problem, store the seeds in a ventilated metal or plastic container. A garbage can works well.

If you need to store your seeds over the summer, keep them in a cool, dry place (in a refrigerator or freezer if possible) to avoid problems with vermin, insects, germination and mold. Do not use seeds that have been stored in a damp area, as they may harbor a lethal mold.

## SEED FEEDER DESIGNS

Seeds can be dispensed from a variety of feeders. Choose one that will require minimum maintenance. It should be easy to fill and should be large enough to hold plenty of seeds. While most bird feeding books recommend using unbreakable plastic rather than glass, Tom Webb of Turner Valley has used glass exclusively in all his feeders for the past several years and has had no problems. Plastic, he points out, degrades in sunlight and has a tendency to bulge, scratch and break in the cold. Whether you choose glass or plastic, make sure the feeder is properly and securely mounted so that it will not blow against a window or crash to the ground. If plastic is used, choose an unbreakable kind which is tougher for squirrels to chew and destroy.

If you are concerned about the health of the trees in your backyard, avoid nailing feeders directly on to them. Instead, attach the feeders with nylon rope, leather or other strapping material. If wire is used, wrap it around a split section of garden hose or rubber. Be sure to loosen the strapping each year so it won't inhibit tree growth.

All seed feeders should be washed in hot, soapy water at least once a year.

### GROUND FEEDING STATIONS

The simplest and least expensive, albeit somewhat wasteful, way to serve seed is simply to scatter it on the ground. Many birds, including redpolls, jays, native sparrows, juncos and grouse prefer to be served their food this way. The Newnhams of Red Deer have a very popular cracked corn and barley ground feeding station that is visited daily during the winter by pheasants and Ruffed Grouse. The Underwoods of Pine Lake report that their ground feeding station of chopped barley and oats is visited regularly during the winter by both grouse and chickadees.

One problem with ground feeding stations is that they often attract cats. To minimize danger from cats, set up your ground feeding station at least 3 m (10 ft) from shrubbery or other places where a cat can hide while stalking the birds. If the feeding station is adjacent to shrubbery, set up low garden fencing or enclose the ground feeder with wire mesh to deter cats.

Despite potential problems with cats, shrubbery is needed to provide both protective cover from predators and shelter from rain, snow and wind. If the area near your ground feeder lacks shrubbery, create some by setting out your old Christmas tree or by building a brush pile.

If you have evergreens in your yard, scatter some seeds beneath the branches as this area rarely gets covered up by snow. If you don't have evergreens, scatter the seeds beneath your parked vehicles, especially when it is snowing.

If you want to minimize wastage, offer the seeds on a surface such as split logs, plywood or fine wire mesh blankets.

## TRAY FEEDERS

Tray feeders, made from plywood, wooden salad bowls, garbage can lids or even old hubcaps, are inexpensive and efficient seed dispensers that can be placed on the ground or on a raised stand. The problem with this style of feeder is that the seeds are exposed to potentially-contaminated bird droppings and to the elements. During a heavy snowstorm they get covered up and when it rains they get wet and soggy. Soggy seeds are unpalatable and often harbor a dangerous mold. To get around this problem, use a fine wire mesh for the floor and/or add a roof.

George Flewwelling of Lacombe uses a large seed starter tray (available at garden centres) for the base of his tray feeders. These trays can easily be removed for cleaning (see bottom right).

Larger tray feeders tend to be better utilized, since more birds can find spots to dine. This helps to reduce the amount of aggressive behavior that is often exhibited when birds are over-crowded on a smaller tray.

## EXCLUSION FEEDERS

Exclusion feeders allow entrance only to smaller birds. This is a preferred design if larger birds are consuming inordinate amounts of seed or are continually denying smaller species access to the feeder. Many feeder operators use exclusion feeders in addition to regular ones, which allows all species to get their fair share. Most covered tray or hopper feeders can be turned into exclusion feeders by enclosing the sides with 3.8 cm (1.5 in) or 5 cm (2 in) stucco wire.

Evening Grosbeaks, usually excluded by the finer mesh, can easily enter and exit through the coarser gauge wire.

## HOPPER FEEDERS

The most efficient seed feeders are those that use a hopper design. These are available in a wide assortment of styles and sizes. Most, like those shown to the right, are quite easy to make in the home workshop.

Hopper feeders offer protection from the elements and hold plenty of seeds if large in size - a real advantage if you don't want to be bothered filling them every day or so. Trays on two or more sides also allow smaller or subordinate birds to feed with the larger dominant ones, as the former can slip in unnoticed to feed on the opposite side of the feeder.

To prevent birds from getting into and contaminating the seed tray with their droppings, make it very narrow and provide perches. To discourage the larger species, simply make the perches too close to the hopper or the feeder tray too narrow for them to perch on.

Hopper feeders can be mounted on wooden posts or metal poles, or hung from a tree or railing bracket. If you use a tree branch, make sure it is a large, solid one. Smaller branches should be avoided as they tend to sway in the wind. This increases the effect of the breeze on the feeder and can cause it to swing enough to scatter the seed. If you mount a feeder on a post or pole, make sure it is high enough off the ground to discourage cats and squirrels. Agile cats and dexterous squirrels can be further discouraged by using baffles (see page 56).

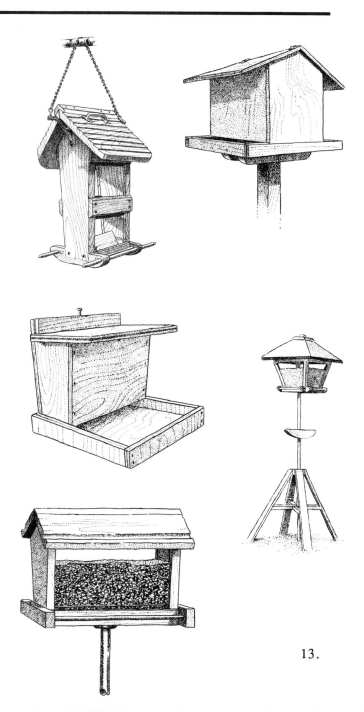

## TUBE AND BOWL FEEDERS

Plastic tube (silo) and bowl feeders are also popular seed dispensers. The seeds are clearly displayed in these feeders and the birds have to reach in to acquire them. This prevents much of the spillage that often occurs with tray or hopper feeders.

The better quality commercial tube feeders have metal-reinforced perches and portals, although they should still be protected with baffles if squirrels are likely to be a problem. Some tube feeders are specifically designed for small birds, with perches too small for larger birds to sit on.

Commercial tube feeders are the most popular, although homemade ones can be easily constructed from plastic mailing tubes or PVC or ABS pipe.

Tube and bowl feeders are usually hung from a bracket or tree branch.

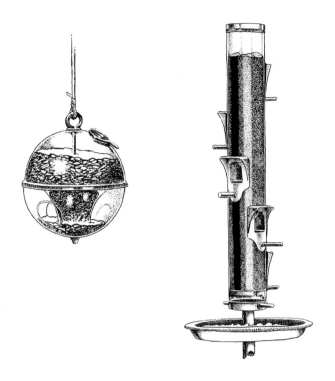

## WINDOW FEEDERS

If you want to watch the birds feeding while you enjoy your morning cup of coffee, try using one of the window feeder designs shown below.

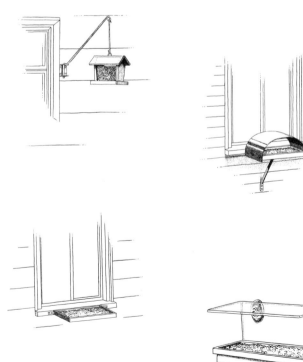

## COMBINATION FEEDERS

Many feeder operators use combination seed or seed/suet feeders. Combination seed/suet feeders usually consist of a hopper feeder with a suet dispenser attached to one end.

Dorothy and David Dickson of Innisfail have designed a combination seed feeder by setting a hopper feeder in the middle of a large tray feeder. They then set this combination on a 1 m (3 ft) triangle of heavy wire mesh (see below). Seeds are placed on the ground inside the triangle to exclude the larger birds and to save the redpolls and chickadees from the cat.

# SEED FEEDERS CHILDREN CAN MAKE

Winter bird feeding programs can be fun and educational for children, who are often keen on making their own feeders. Thoroughly cleaned ice cream pails, coffee cans, old dishes, pie plates, milk cartons, coconut shells, small boxes and clean plastic bottles and jugs can all be used. Since most of these materials are light and will blow around in the wind, make sure they are securely fastened to a tree or feeder stand, or at least weighted or anchored with a rock. If cans or other metal containers are used, be sure to tape any exposed edges to prevent injury to the birds or the children.

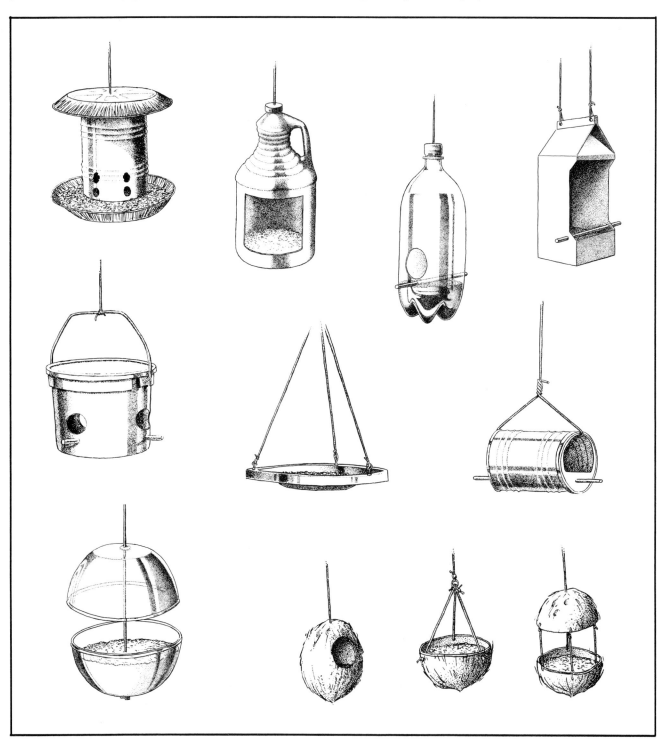

# SEED FEEDER STANDS

While feeders can be set on the corner of the balcony or on the ground, both the seeds and the birds will be safer if the feeders are either hung from a branch or mounted on a free-standing structure.

The most secure method for building a stand is to drive a 2.5 or 5 cm (1 or 2 in) pipe or a 10 x 10 cm (4 x 4 in) treated post into the ground 0.5 m (1.5 ft) deep, then mount the feeder on top of it. Although this will provide a secure support structure for the feeder, you're stuck with a pipe or a post in your yard all year round. A solution to this problem is to make a small concrete pad with a hole in the centre into which the feeder pole can be set; the pole can then be removed when not in use.

If you want to be able to move your feeders at the end of the season, mount them on portable stands. Marie Pijeau of Sylvan Lake reports success using portable stands braced by support "feet" (see bottom left). For small feeders, she uses 45 cm (18 in) feet to support 5 x 5 cm (2 x 2 in) posts. Large feeders are supported by 60 cm (24 in) feet and 10 x 10 cm (4 x 4 in) posts. Tom Webb of Turner Valley uses umbrella-style support feet for his large seed feeders. Railing brackets and metal support feet are also very effective and are available commercially.

If you want to be able to adjust the height of your feeder stands, consider using telescoping poles (the kind used to run power cords above sidewalks during the winter), which are also available commercially.

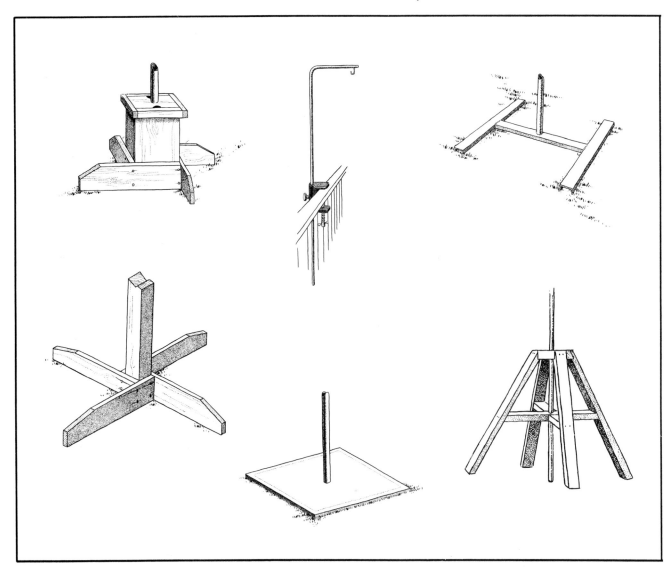

# TYPES OF SEED

There are about a dozen different types of seeds that can be offered to birds. Some of the most popular ones are listed here, in order of preference.

## SUNFLOWER SEEDS

Sunflower seeds are the most sought after of all feeder seeds, which is not surprising considering their high fat and protein content. Sunflower seeds supply more energy than most other seeds found in the wild (Manitoba maple, for example) or even most insect larvae.

There are two varieties of sunflower seeds commonly available in Alberta: the large, striped and the small, black oilseed. The oilseed variety has a thinner hull, is easier for small birds to manipulate and contains more oil per gram than the striped variety, but is actually harder for some birds to crack open. Feeder operators in Alberta are divided as to which type of seed is preferable. Many in the northern and central parts of the province swear by the oilseed variety while others, especially those in the southern parts of the province, report that the small seeds are completely ignored by all species in favor of the striped variety! *Which seeds do your birds prefer? Please let us know!*

If you grow sunflowers in your garden, set out the ripened heads on a tray feeder. Several species, especially jays and cross-bills, will pick the seeds directly from it.

The most popular way to present sunflower seeds is to offer the whole (shelled or unshelled) seed. Unshelled ones can also be served ground or chopped-up using a meat grinder, food processor or blender. Redpolls, siskins and chickadees are especially fond of ground sunflower seeds. If it is too difficult to offer on a daily basis, at least try to serve them in extremely cold weather. This saves the birds from having to expend the extra energy required to crack open or scrounge through the seeds.

You can cut down on wastage around your sunflower seed feeder by using screen or 3 mm (1/8 in) hardware cloth, raised slightly off the ground, beneath it. Spilled and tossed-out seeds land on the screen, keeping them drier and cleaner than if they land directly on the ground. It also makes them readily available to the ground-feeding birds.

Offering only shelled sunflower seeds is more expensive, but it saves the messy job of raking up sunflower seed hulls every spring.

Sunflower seeds can be dispensed from a variety of feeders, including trays, hoppers and tubes. Avoid serving them on the ground because they'll get soggy and many will germinate in the spring!

BIRDS ATTRACTED TO UNSHELLED SUNFLOWER SEEDS: Red-winged and Rusty Blackbird, Black-capped and Mountain Chickadee, Red and White-winged Crossbill, Cassin's, House and Purple Finch, American Goldfinch, Evening and Pine Grosbeak, Blue, Gray and Steller's Jay, Black-billed Magpie, Clark's Nutcracker, Red-breasted and White-breasted Nuthatch, Common and Hoary Redpoll, Pine Siskin, House Sparrow, Downy and Hairy Woodpecker.

BIRDS ATTRACTED TO SHELLED SUNFLOWER SEEDS: all of the above, plus Snow Bunting, Boreal Chickadee, Rosy Finch, Dark-eyed Junco, Chipping, Fox, Harris', Golden-crowned, Lincoln's and White-throated Sparrow, Rufous-sided Towhee.

## NIGER SEED

This tiny black seed from a tropical thistle plant is an expensive favorite of the finch family. It will not grow in our rigorous Alberta climate, so you don't have to worry about it becoming a nuisance in your yard. Niger seed is an excellent source of fat and protein but is so expensive that you will likely want to dispense it from a special tube feeder that has small openings (see below). These small holes will keep wastage to a minimum and will prevent some species, especially House Sparrows, from having access to the seed.

BIRDS ATTRACTED TO NIGER SEED: Red and White-winged Crossbill, House and Purple Finch, American Goldfinch, Dark-eyed Junco, Common and Hoary Redpoll, Pine Siskin, House Sparrow, Song and White-throated Sparrow.

## CANOLA

Canola is also a popular feeder seed that is eagerly consumed by finches. If you purchase canola seed from a seed supplier, make sure that it is untreated. Treated seed is highly toxic and may be recognized by its bright, uniform pink or purple color. Untreated seed contains a variety of colors ranging from yellow to black. While you may be able to acquire uncleaned seed, free of charge, from farmers or at grain elevators, be warned that the weed seeds mixed in with the canola are often noxious and can quickly spread to cultivated areas throughout your (and your neighbor's) yard.

Canola can be dispensed from almost any feeder, although the tube-style is most often used.

BIRDS ATTRACTED TO CANOLA: Cassin's, House and Purple Finch, American Goldfinch, Common and Hoary Redpoll, Pine Siskin, Song Sparrow.

## NUTS

Nuts are nutritious but expensive, so most people offer them sparingly. If squirrels ever discover that you arc scrving nuts, they will go to great lengths to feast on these delicacies. You may end up having to pit your ingenuity against their persistence if you hope to discourage them!

Peanuts are the most popular nuts, appealing to many insect and seed eating birds because of their high fat and protein content. Shelled or unshelled, they are a favorite of the Blue Jay. In addition to serving whole peanuts in tray or hopper-style feeders, they can be tied together with a string or skewered on to a piece of galvanized wire and hung from a tree branch.

Peanut butter, one of the most sought-after feeder foods, has been (probably incorrectly) implicated in the choking deaths of a few birds. To be on the safe side, especially in warm weather, mix peanut butter with suet (any proportion) or cornmeal (1 part cornmeal to 3-5 parts peanut butter) to ensure that it can be swallowed safely.

Walnuts are also a favorite. Winnie Ellis of Lacombe reports that walnuts are especially favored by the chickadees, robins and White-crowned Sparrows at her feeders. The McCulloughs of Calgary serve walnut pieces to their chickadees from a small clay feeder with two access holes small enough to prevent House Sparrows from entering it (see below). They string the feeder on a wire so it is well away from any perching place large enough to accommodate squirrels. On both sides of the feeder, they string a series of short pieces of thin plastic tubing that rolls and dislodges anything larger than a small bird.

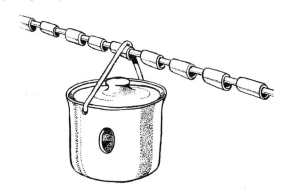

While an occasional meal of salted nuts will probably not harm your feeder birds, you should use unsalted ones if you are planning to provide them as a steady diet.

BIRDS ATTRACTED TO NUTS: Black-capped, Boreal and Mountain Chickadee, American Crow, Evening Grosbeak, Blue and Steller's Jay, Black-billed Magpie, Clark's Nutcracker, Red-breasted and White-breasted Nuthatch, Common Raven, Common and Hoary Redpoll, Chipping, Fox, Tree, White-crowned and White-throated Sparrow, European Starling, Rufous-sided Towhee, Bohemian and Cedar Waxwing, Downy and Hairy Woodpecker.

## CORN

Corn is rich in carbohydrates and is a good source of vitamin A. Whole kernel corn is a favorite of the Blue Jay, but cracked corn seems to be preferred more by House Sparrows than any other species. If House Sparrows have not yet plagued your feeders, it would probably be best to avoid using corn. If House Sparrows are not likely to be a problem, rolled or cracked corn will be readily consumed by several species. If you have Ruffed Grouse, Sharp-tailed Grouse, Gray Partridges or Ring-necked Pheasants over-wintering in your area, you may entice them to your backyard by offering them coarse cracked corn.

Corn can be served right from the cob or from tray or ground feeders. It can be offered whole, cracked or rolled, or finely-ground and mixed with ground wheat (called chick scratch). Avoid dispensing it from hopper feeders, as it is very absorbent and will easily go moldy and clog the feeder.

BIRDS ATTRACTED TO CORN: Mourning Dove, Northern Flicker, Evening Grosbeak, Ruffed and Sharp-tailed Grouse, Blue and Steller's Jay, Dark-eyed Junco, White-breasted Nuthatch, Gray Partridge, Ring-necked Pheasant, Common and Hoary Redpoll, American Robin, House Sparrow, Fox, Savannah and White-throated Sparrow, Rufous-sided Towhee, Wild Turkey.

## WHITE MILLET

White millet is a good seed to serve either alone or mixed with other small seeds. Because it has a hard seed coat, which resists swelling and rotting, it can be dispensed from hopper or tube feeders without clogging the openings. Hardy Pletz reports that this is a favorite food of the redpolls at his feeders near Wetaskiwin, while Bea Ross of Black Diamond and Jean McCullough of Calgary report that it is favored more by House Sparrows than by any other species at their feeders.

BIRDS ATTRACTED TO WHITE MILLET: Snow Bunting, Rosy Finch, House, Cassin's and Purple Finch, Dark-eyed Junco, Common and Hoary Redpoll, House Sparrow, Chipping, Fox, Harris', Lincoln's, Savannah, Song, White-crowned and White-throated Sparrow, European Starling, Rufous-sided Towhee.

## WEED SEEDS

In areas where they protrude above the snow, weeds are an important food source for many over-wintering bird species. If you aren't worried about the possibility of them spreading around your yard, collect non-noxious weeds (Pigweed, Lamb's Quarter, Knotweed and Ragweed) after they have set seed. During the winter, shake out the seeds on to tray feeders. If you aren't sure which weeds are noxious, contact your local District Agriculturist or County Agricultural Fieldman and ask for a copy of the Weed Control Act, Weed Designation Regulation #138-80.

BIRDS ATTRACTED TO WEED SEEDS: Snow Bunting, Mourning Dove, American Goldfinch, Dark-eyed Junco, Common and Hoary Redpoll, Chipping, Clay-colored, Lincoln's, Savannah, Song, Tree and White-crowned Sparrow.

## CANARY SEED

This is an expensive seed that is readily eaten, but less preferred than even white millet.

BIRDS ATTRACTED TO CANARY SEED: Dark-eyed Junco, Rosy Finch, White-crowned and White-throated Sparrow, Rufous-sided Towhee.

## SAFFLOWER

Safflower seeds appear to be becoming more popular as a feeder food. They are not favored by Gray Squirrels, which may be an advantage if you live in an area where they are a nuisance.

BIRDS ATTRACTED TO SAFFLOWER SEEDS: Purple Finch, Evening Grosbeak, Blue Jay, Ring-necked Pheasant.

## VEGETABLE AND FRUIT SEEDS

Most seed-eating species will dine on the seeds of pumpkins, cantaloupes, watermelons and squash. Just wash, dry and serve.

BIRDS ATTRACTED TO VEGETABLE AND FRUIT SEEDS: Black-capped, Boreal and Mountain Chickadee, Purple Finch, Blue Jay, Red-breasted and White-breasted Nuthatch.

## SEEDS TO AVOID

Commercial seed mixtures and cereal grains (wheat, oats, rice, milo, buckwheat, millets other than white) are rejected by most desirable feeder species. Studies have shown that most supermarket bird seed contains a high percentage of red milo (grain sorghum), a filler material that is ignored by most birds. Furthermore, red milo and hulled oats are favorites of European Starlings, while wheat is eagerly sought after by House Sparrows. For these reasons, avoid using commercial birdseed unless you can have control over the contents of the mixture.

Feeder operators who live near water are sometimes able to attract waterfowl by offering them wheat or barley. Jean McCullough of Calgary serves wheat to the waterfowl in her backyard during the summer by setting it underwater on a shallow ledge. Make sure the grains you use have not been chemically treated.

# THE IMPORTANCE OF GRIT

All seed-eating birds require a gizzard full of abrasive material to crush and grind the seeds before digestion can take place. Grit is often difficult for them to find in the winter, especially after a snowfall, so it should be added as a feeder food supplement. Commercial grit, beach sand or crushed charcoal can be offered from a separate feeder or added directly to the seeds (about a handful per ice-cream bucket). Birds will also consume the grit and salt that falls from parked vehicles in the winter.

# ATTRACTING WINTER BIRDS WITH SUET, GOURMET TREATS, WATER

Downy (left) and Hairy Woodpecker

Boreal Chickadee

# ATTRACTING BIRDS WITH SUET

Suet and fat are high energy foods eagerly sought by birds that eat insects in the summer (fat and insects are made of similar stuff). Suet is the hard fat found around the kidneys and heart of cattle and sheep, while regular fat occurs throughout an animal's body and is obtained by trimming beef, lamb or pork cuts. Beef suet is very popular while pork fat is generally considered to be a somewhat less palatable offering. Both suet and beef fat can be obtained from supermarket meat counters or from butcher shops. Ground suet (used in plum pudding) is also readily available.

Although a certain amount of salt is essential for all birds, excessive amounts may cause paralysis of the nervous system. For this reason, avoid using the drippings from bacon or other processed meats.

For simplicity's sake, both suet and fat will be referred to as suet in this text.

## SUET FEEDER DESIGNS

A suet feeding station can range from the simple to the elegant. The easiest and most popular method is to hang a piece of raw suet, enclosed in an onion or other nylon mesh bag, from a tree branch. Make sure the bag is kept full, as the birds may get tangled in it if it is partially empty. Wire mesh bags and soap dishes also work well. The warning that metal dispensers should be avoided because the birds will freeze to it, is unfounded; birds' feet are covered with dry, horny scales which allow them to perch comfortably on metal even in extremely cold temperatures. Healthy birds have such quick reaction times that it is unlikely that their eyes or tongues would ever touch the metal. If you use metal feeders, be sure to turn down or tape all sharp metal edges so the birds don't get cut.

If you serve pork fat, put it out with the rind still attached. Nail it to a post or wall, wire it on to a tree trunk or branch, or make a slit in the hide and slip it over a broken branch.

# GOURMET SUET FEEDING

If you would like to add a gourmet flair to your suet feeding, try rendering the suet and mixing it with other delectable delights. To render, cut the suet up into small pieces or put it through a meat grinder. Melt small quantities at a time in an oven at 120°C (250°F), in a microwave, frying pan or in the bottom of a pressure cooker pot (lid off/element or burner set on medium). Strain out the rind and other impurities by pouring it through a metal sieve or colander lined with cheese cloth. If you want to add peanut butter, do so while the suet is still hot, then set the mixture to cool in a safe place. If you want really smooth suet, repeat the melt/cool process twice. When it becomes the consistency of butter, mix in the remaining ingredients and spread on to tree trunks or spoon into suet logs, suet sticks, cup cake cases or pine cones.

Recommended additions to suet include bran, currants, whole wheat flour, cottage cheese, raisins, dates, figs, chopped nuts, honey (only when outside temperatures are below freezing), barley flakes, corn oil, moist coconut (dry coconut, which will expand after ingestion, can be lethal), cracked or rolled corn, grated or small cubes of cheese, pieces of apple and crabapple, bread crumbs, Nanking cherries, mountain ash berries, Mayday berries, snowberries, blueberries, cranberries, saskatoons, dried ground meat, grit, coal ashes or finely crushed eggshells, rolled oats, cornbread, cornmeal, cream of wheat, wheat germ, crumbled dog food, cat food, dried or stale pastry, gerbil food, hard boiled eggs (mashed), rabbit pellets, hamster pellets, popcorn, chopped cooked noodles and graham crackers.

Suet cake, made from a base mixture of suet, fat, vegetable shortening or lard, then mixed with flour, peanut butter and cornmeal is also eagerly consumed.

A sugar-based suet mixture may also be used. Make a sugar syrup by boiling a solution of 1 part sugar to 4 parts water. Add the syrup to a mixture of suet, peanut butter, flour and cornmeal. Form into balls and serve.

If you or your neighbors use a "bug zapper" (not recommended, by the way, because they destroy all nocturnal insects) during the summer, collect and freeze the dead insects to add to the suet mixture. If you are really enthusiastic, you may also consider collecting and freezing ant eggs during the summer for your winter suet mixtures. Other novel additions could include the eggs, larvae, etc. from old wasp and hornet nests, freeze-dried insects (the kind used for tropical fish) and mealworms (see page 24 for instructions on how to raise them).

Though it is often recommended, it is not a good idea to mix hard-shelled seeds and suet together. Few species enjoy both and, while the suet lovers can ignore the seeds, the seed-eaters will have difficulty opening grease-coated seeds and may spread fat on their feathers while attempting to do so.

When the warm temperatures of spring begin to melt the suet in your feeders and turn it rancid, you may want to substitute an all-season concoction of vegetable shortening, peanut butter, cornmeal and flour. While some naturalists warn that rancid suet mats the feathers and may actually be harmful to the birds, many feeder operators in Alberta report that, as long as all the meat is removed, the birds relish both the rancid suet and the maggots that grow in it. Kerry and Marjorie Wood of Red Deer report that woodpeckers come to their suet feeders throughout the year, with no apparent ill effects. The woodpeckers even bring their young with them to dine on the dripping, rancid suet in mid-summer.

BIRDS ATTRACTED TO SUET STATIONS: Black-capped, Boreal and Mountain Chickadee, Brown Creeper, American Crow, Northern Flicker, Golden-crowned Kinglet, Blue and Gray Jay, Black-billed Magpie, Clark's Nutcracker, Red-breasted and White-breasted Nuthatch, Common Raven, Hairy, Downy and Pileated Woodpecker, European Starling.

If you wish to protect your suet feeders from squirrels, magpies and starlings, see page 55.

# BONE SAWDUST

Bone sawdust is generated during the process of butchering an animal. It is relished by all suet eaters and is certainly a favorite food of the Brown Creeper. If you have spruce trees in or near your backyard, a supply of bone sawdust will likely entice this elusive bird to become a regular patron.

Maintaining a bone sawdust station takes a bit more care and attention than does a regular suet station. In its raw state, bone sawdust is very crumbly and friable. The best way to serve it is to smear it on the trunks of spruce trees with a wooden spoon or spatula. Apply in an upward motion, as Brown Creepers generally travel up a tree trunk. Bone sawdust will rot within a matter of hours under warm conditions, so serve it only when outside temperatures are well below freezing.

Another option is to form fresh sawdust into small balls which can be immediately frozen, then set out in mesh bags or other suet holders as required. Since Brown Creepers appear to have difficulty figuring out how to eat from a free-hanging feeder, make sure some of the bone sawdust is served directly on a tree trunk if you want to attract them. As long as it is fresh, bone sawdust can also be mixed with regular suet and included in other suet recipes.

BIRDS ATTRACTED TO BONE SAWDUST: Black-capped, Boreal and Mountain Chickadee, Brown Creeper, Northern Flicker, Blue and Gray Jay, Black-billed Magpie, Red-breasted and White-breasted Nuthatch.

Magpies will go to great lengths to eat bone sawdust and will quickly figure out how to eat it directly off the tree trunk. To prevent magpies from dining at your bone sawdust stations, use exclusion feeders (see page 55) or restrict your stations to the small, free-hanging variety.

# SUET RECIPES

The following recipes are just three of hundreds that have been developed for bird feeding. Try your own concoctions, too!

## PINE CONE FILLING
250 ml (1 cup) melted suet
125 ml (1/2 cup) peanut butter
125 ml (1/2 cup) cornmeal and chopped raisins
125 ml (1/2 cup) rolled oats
125 ml (1/2 cup) wheat germ
125 ml (1/2 cup) crushed walnuts
small handful of grit
Mix together and spoon into five large pine cones. Store in freezer until needed.

## CHICKADEE TREAT
500 g (1 lb) melted suet
375 g (12 oz) peanut butter
500 ml (2 cups) rolled oats
125 ml (1/2 cup) barley flakes or moist coconut
875 ml (3 1/2 cups) cornmeal mixed with bran
1 l (4 1/2 cups) water
875 ml (3 1/2 cups) oatmeal
875 ml (3 1/2 cups) cream of wheat
Mix and spoon on to suet sticks or suet logs. Store in freezer until needed.

## SUET CUPCAKES
Cook 500 ml (2 cups) of oatmeal in 1 litre (4 1/2 cups) of boiling water for two minutes. Add 500 g (1 lb) of lard or melted suet, 375 g (12 oz) of peanut butter, a handful of chopped figs or dates and a cubed apple. Mix thoroughly. Remove from heat and stir in 50 ml (1/4 cup) cottage cheese and 875 ml (3 1/2 cups) each of dry oatmeal, cornmeal and cream of wheat. Put into cup cake cases. Freeze and serve as required.

## GROWING MEALWORMS

Fill an ice cream pail, aquarium, glass jar or other smooth-walled container half full with a mixture of bran, bread crumbs, cornmeal or crushed crackers. Mix in 25-50 mealworm larvae, available at most fishing and pet stores. On top, place a few thin slices of apple or tomato. Finally, cover everything with several layers of newspaper. Be sure to cover the container with a tight but well-ventilated lid. It takes about three months for the larvae to transform to adult beetles and for the adults to lay eggs. When adults have emerged, move them to a new container with a new supply of bran, sliced apple and newspaper.

# ATTRACTING BIRDS WITH GOURMET TREATS

## PASTRY

Pastry consists of ground grains and fat (shortening), both of which birds relish. Unfortunately, the birds that usually arrive first at a bread or doughnut-laden feeder are House Sparrows and starlings. If you aren't yet troubled by these two species, it would probably be best to avoid using pastry as feeder food. On the other hand, if you have a flock of sparrows or starlings that are keeping other birds away from the seed feeders, you may want to set out the bread away from the main feeders to entice these competitors away.

Joan Susut of Lacombe has found that bran muffins are an irresistible treat for Boreal Chickadees. During the winter of 1988-89, Tom Webb of Turner Valley had a Brown Thrasher spend the entire season at his feeders. While it did eat ground sunflower seeds and the occasional saskatoon berry, it preferred (and lived the whole winter on) pie pastry! Dave Elphinstone reports that a Cape May Warbler once stayed in Calgary until January at a feeder that offered Christmas cake and peanut butter. Winnie Ellis of Lacombe reports that her cornbread is relished by Black-capped Chickadees during the winter, by Savannah and White-crowned Sparrows in the spring and by robins during the spring and summer.

BIRDS ATTRACTED TO PASTRY: Black-capped, Mountain and Boreal Chickadee, American Crow, Blue, Gray and Steller's Jay, Black-billed Magpie, White-breasted and Red-breasted Nuthatch, Common Raven, Common and Hoary Redpoll, American Robin, House Sparrow, Savannah and White-crowned Sparrow, European Starling, Downy Woodpecker.

## FRUIT AND BERRIES

Fruit and berries are appealing to those birds which eat insects and/or fruit during the spring and summer. Cubes of dried (a home food dehydrater works well) or frozen bananas, oranges, apples, pears, plums, peaches, cherries as well as dates, figs, raisins (soaked) and currants are all popular with several bird species. Berries (elder, saskatoon, dogwood, mountain ash, Nanking cherry, chokecherry, Mayday, snowberry and cotoneaster) may also be offered.

If you continue to feed fruit into the spring and summer, you may also attract such summer birds as orioles, tanagers, warblers, catbirds and thrashers to your feeders.

BIRDS ATTRACTED TO FRUIT: Ruffed Grouse, Blue and Gray Jay, Black-billed Magpie, American Robin, Cedar and Bohemian Waxwing, Hairy Woodpecker.

## THE ODD AND UNUSUAL

Charis Cooper of Turner Valley serves her birds a couple of novel food items, both of which have proven to be great hits. In the fall, she retrieves old wasp and hornet nests. During the winter, she breaks them apart and sets them out on a tray feeder. The chickadees love to pick through the nests looking for eggs, larvae, etc. She also hangs out left-over chicken and turkey carcasses for the birds to pick away at. Gray Jays and chickadees love to glean bits of frozen meat and peck at the bones of these carcasses.

Other novel offerings include cooked sweet potatoes and vermicelli for robins, a mixture of peanut butter and baked beans for chickadees and boiled potatoes for Brown Creepers.

Tom Webb, also of Turner Valley, claims that salmon-flavored cat food is a definite favorite of several of his feeder birds. Cal Lockhart of Lac La Biche has found that dog food is relished by Blue Jays - to the point that they will virtually ignore the sunflower seeds and peanuts in the other feeders. Other pet foods that will be eaten include rabbit pellets and gerbil food.

In the spring, especially after a snowstorm, you may try offering live mealworm larvae, which will be eagerly devoured by most bird species. Offer them in a shallow glass tray or smooth, metal-walled container on a feeding table, or offer them by hand. They're such a great hit that birds will soon come close to you looking for a handout. Unless you grow your own, offering mealworms may become expensive. To grow your own, see facing page.

## CALCIUM

You may consider supplementing your feeder birds' calcium intake by providing ground oyster shell or crushed eggshells. To offer eggshells, simply collect them in a tin can or glass jar. When the can or jar is full, dry the shells in the oven on low heat for about 10 minutes. When the shells are brittle, pulverize them finely. Crushed egg shells can be served alone on ground or tray feeders, added to suet mixtures or mixed in with seeds.

# ATTRACTING BIRDS WITH WATER

One very important, but often overlooked, technique for attracting winter birds (even the non-feeder species) into your backyard is to provide them with water. Most wild birds must resort to eating snow in order to get their needed fluids during the winter months. While this doesn't seem to be a great hardship, birds are readily attracted to a source of drinking and bathing water all year round. Jean McCullough has watched Bohemian Waxwings and House Sparrows bathe merrily away in her baths in Calgary at -35°C!

One inexpensive but time-consuming method of providing water is to keep filling the bath with a kettle of hot water. Don't use water that has boiled, as it actually freezes more quickly than unboiled water. While this technique may work reasonably well on warm days, it is quite futile in extremely cold conditions.

The other option is to heat the baths electrically. If you choose this method, keep in mind all safety precautions. George Flewwelling of Lacombe designed the electrically-heated winter bird bath shown below.

He constructed this bath by mounting a large one-way disk blade on a metal stand. He welded a metal tube to the bottom of the disk, then inserted a 50 watt light bulb and fiberglass insulation. The water stays open in this bath to about -20°C.

Both Jean McCullough of Calgary and Winnie Ellis of Lacombe report success using old electric frying pans (with the heat on low, of course!) for winter bird baths.

Doug Meston of Rocky Mountain House has designed an inexpensive, easily-constructed bath that keeps water open even in -40°C temperatures.

The only materials required for this bath (shown below) are six pieces of 18.5 mm (3/4 in) plywood, a shallow dish (the drip tray from a large flower pot works well), an extension cord with a light bulb attachment (or a cord and a junction box if you want to get sophisticated), some fiberglass insulation, a large aluminum can and a 25 watt (for milder weather) or a 50 watt (for extremely cold temperatures) "rough service" light bulb.

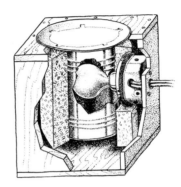

Dimensions
Floor: 30.5 x 30.5 cm
(12 x 12 in)
2 Sides: 34.3 x 33 cm
(13.5 x 13 in)
2 Sides: 30.5 x 33 cm
(12 x 13 in)
Top: 34.3 x 34.3 cm
(13.5 x 13.5 in)
Hole: 27.9 cm (11 in)
Bulb should be placed
15.3 cm (6 in) below bottom
of water dish.

Commercially-available heated bird baths are becoming increasingly popular, and are now readily available in Alberta at nature centres, nature stores in Calgary and Edmonton, or pet stores that carry bird seed. Heaters are also available by mail-order (see list of periodicals on page 64).

Commercial bird baths come in a variety of styles. Some are simply pans wrapped with heat tape while others use submersible heaters or floating de-icers. The disadvantage with the heat tape variety of bath is the lack of thermostatic control, which can be a problem if the pan becomes completely empty between refills. There are also varieties that can be used unheated during the summer, then plugged in when needed during the winter. Jean McCullough, who has used several styles of water heaters in her bird baths in Calgary, advises that all heaters will eventually corrode and break apart if an anode rod is not set in the water beside them.

Stock tank water heaters can be used in large bird baths. Avoid using aquarium heaters, as they are fragile and do not last in our rigorous climate.

# WHO'S COMING TO DINNER?

Gray  Jay

American  Robin

# WHO'S COMING TO DINNER?

Approximately sixty species of birds can be attracted to feeders in Alberta. Watching these feeder birds is much more enjoyable if they can be identified, and if something is known about their behavior and life-histories.

## BIRD TOPOGRAPHY

Birders use a standardized language when describing the physical characteristics of an individual bird or a bird species. The diagram below describes basic "bird topography".

## THE FASCINATING WORLD OF BIRD BEHAVIOR

Bird feeders provide great opportunities to watch bird behavior. Donald and Lillian Stokes, in their popular *Bird Behavior* books, provide some fascinating insights into how and why birds act the way they do. They warn that we must be careful to avoid interpreting bird behavior by basing our assessments on human feelings and emotions. One good example of a widespread but incorrect belief is that birds sing only when they are happy. Singing is just one of many ritualized behaviors that has evolved to help individual birds reproduce successfully.

Behavior in all animals, including birds, is directed at the survival of the individual and of the species. While instinct plays a large part in determining this preservation behavior, it is believed that many behavioral characteristics are also learned.

Bird behavior is commonly described as being one of two types:

### MAINTENANCE BEHAVIOR

This is behavior birds undertake to maintain their own bodies. Included are activities such as feeding, drinking, bathing (in dust, snow, water, rain and sunlight), scratching, plumage ruffling and shaking, tail-fanning, bill-wiping, sleeping and preening.

### SOCIAL BEHAVIOR

This is behavior birds exhibit for the purpose of communicating to others around them. Social behavior is easily observed at feeders because feeding stations provide a constant, rich food supply in a confined area. Birds attracted to feeders must compete with others of their own flock, as well as with other species, for the right to partake of the offerings. This competition leads to the establishment of a pecking order, with dominant birds acquiring the right to eat their fill before subordinate members may feed. Once this hierarchy is established, the birds spend a minimal amount of time and energy fighting, so are able to turn their full attention to the serious business of keeping their bellies full.

The Stokes have identified four common techniques used by feeder birds to establish and/or maintain their slot in the hierarchy.

*Displacement*: A dominant or larger bird flies at a subordinate or smaller bird and displaces it from its spot. Blue Jays and magpies are expert displacers!

*Head Forward*: The bird stretches forward, pointing its beak (which is often open) at the bird it is challenging. This is often used by a bird when it wants to move a subordinate out of its way. It doesn't always work. Redpolls often exhibit this behavior.

*Crest Raise*: The feathers on the top of the bird's head are temporarily raised. This is often done by a bird that has just arrived at a feeder and is trying to find a dining spot. Crest-raising is especially evident among Purple Finches.

*Wing Droop*: The bird raises its tail slightly while drooping the wingtips. This is a signal of aggression or dominance and is often used in conjunction with the head forward behavior. This conduct is commonly seen among Pine Siskins.

Birds also exhibit "alarm" behavior if a predator approaches. Cats or other ground predators are usually subjected to a harsh scolding as the birds watch them from the safety of a nearby tree. Aerial predators appear to be viewed more seriously. When a warning whistle is issued by one of the flock, all freeze in position and become silent. You can often be alerted to the presence of an owl, hawk or shrike in your yard by this behavior. Some species, especially crows, jays and magpies, will "gang up" and mob a potential predator.

# A DIRECTORY OF FEEDER BIRDS

This section will help you identify the birds that are attracted to winter bird feeding stations in Alberta. Some of the species listed are very common, while others are rare or occasional visitors. All can be expected to visit feeders somewhere in Alberta in late fall, winter or early spring.

The species are listed in taxonomic order, the same as in field guides. A good field guide should be used to complement this section, not only to help identify feeder species but also to help identify other Alberta winter birds that do not use feeders. For a list of field guides, see page 62.

---

## WATERFOWL

Thousands of ducks over-winter in Alberta where water remains open, usually adjacent to industrial sites. They will readily accept offerings of bread, grain and millet. It is not a good idea to feed ducks in the fall, as handouts often unduly delay them from migrating. High waterfowl populations, especially when restricted to limited areas of open water, are subject to outbreaks of cholera and other contagious diseases.

## GROUSE

RUFFED GROUSE
*(Bonasa umbellus)*
SHARP-TAILED GROUSE
*(Tympanuchus phasianellus)*
GRAY (HUNGARIAN) PARTRIDGE
*(Perdix perdix)*
RING-NECKED PHEASANT
*(Phasianus colchicus)*

The Ruffed Grouse is a bird of the deciduous and mixed-wood forests. It is a tame bird that can be identified by its small crest, black ruffs and a multi-banded tail that it fans during the breeding season. Ruffed Grouse can be heard "drumming" their wings in the spring and fall.

The Sharp-tailed Grouse, locally called "Prairie Chicken", is found throughout Alberta, although its numbers have declined in recent years. It is the same size as the Ruffed Grouse, but can be distinguished by its grayish color, pointed tail and orange eye combs.

The Gray Partridge (below right) and Ring-necked Pheasant were both introduced into Alberta as game birds.

The Gray Partridge has adapted well in the central and southern regions of the province and is common year round in most habitats. Pheasants have not fared as well, as they over-winter only in very localized areas of the province and only in habitats that provide adequate cover. Where they have become successfully established, there is evidence to suggest that the Ring-necked Pheasant has displaced the native Sharp-tailed Grouse.

If you see grouse in your area, you may be able to attract them to ground feeders that offer cracked or rolled corn, chopped or whole oats, buckwheat, barley or wheat. Hans Bernes has found that barley is very popular with the flock of 30 Sharp-tails he feeds each winter on his farm near Rimbey.

Wildlife biologists in Minnesota have recently devised feeding stations for Sharp-tailed Grouse that have proven to be as popular as the old straw stacks of the threshing machine era. They should work equally well in Alberta.

A Sharp-tailed feeding station is constructed by stacking six to 12 greenfeed or uncombined grain bales into a pyramid shape. Straw bales can be used for the first tier, which will likely be buried under snow. When the stack is complete, all the strings are cut to allow it to fall apart. The grouse are then able to use the stack for both feeding and burrowing into for cover. The stack should be placed at the edge of a clearing, preferably near a wooded area of mixed spruce and poplar. *We would be interested in hearing from anyone who has used this technique.*

## WILD TURKEY
*(Meleagris gallopavo)*
The Wild Turkey, ancestor to our domestic turkey, was introduced into Alberta in the 1960s and '70s. A few pockets of them still remain in the Porcupine and Cypress Hills and around Turner Valley.

The Lethbridge Fish and Game Association has developed a supplemental feeding program for the turkeys in the Porcupine Hills. Harold Janecke, who was instrumental in initiating the project, reports that they feed on oats and other cereal grains, lentils, corn and buckwheat.

# DOVES

## ROCK DOVE
*(Columba livia)*
Rock Doves are more commonly referred to as pigeons. Introduced from Europe by early settlers, they are now widespread and common. They have adapted so well in urban areas that they are often seen as pests.

Pigeons will be attracted to ground feeders that offer the same foods attractive to House Sparrows - grain, popcorn and bread scraps.

## MOURNING DOVE
*(Zenaida macroura)*
The Mourning Dove is a trim-bodied bird with a long, tapering tail and a pinkish wash on its underparts. Most leave the province by early October and arrive back in late April or early May.

Mourning Doves aren't common feeder birds in Alberta, but you may be able to attract them in the spring or fall by offering grain or cracked corn from ground feeders.

# WOODPECKERS

Woodpeckers are found wherever there are trees. Their habit of pecking, whether looking for food, excavating nest cavities, beating out territorial calls or advertising for a mate, requires very specialized adaptations. Sharp, hard beaks are powered by massive neck muscles. Thick bristles around their nostrils filter out the sawdust. Long and extendible tongues are equipped with sticky saliva and/or barbs to extract insects or brush up sap. Their brains are protected by a thin cushion of air within thick, reinforced skulls. Woodpeckers are adept at clinging to the trunk of a tree with the aid of a stiff tail and sharp, specialized toes (two toes pointing forward and one or two back). All woodpeckers fly in a characteristic undulating pattern.

## NORTHERN FLICKER
### (Colaptes auratus)

Alberta's only brown woodpecker, the Northern Flicker has a black crescent-shaped bib and a white rump that is conspicuous in flight. Only the males have a red or black moustachial stripe. There are two subspecies of Northern Flickers in Alberta: Red-shafted and Yellow-shafted.

A few Northern Flickers over-winter in Alberta each year, and will sometimes visit a backyard feeder to dine on cracked corn, suet or bone sawdust. They also seem to like bacon drippings.

## DOWNY WOODPECKER
### (Picoides pubescens)

The smallest of our Alberta woodpeckers, Downys are commonly found in poplar groves and wooded coulees during the winter. They are smaller than their similar-looking cousin, the Hairy, have much shorter bills (shorter than the distance between the eye and the back of the head) and have black spots on the white outer tail feathers. Females lack the bright red nape patch of the male.

Female Downys wander farther than the males during the winter, so are likely to be the more common of the two at your feeder. If you have Hairy Woodpeckers around, make sure you set out more than one feeding station well apart from each other, as the Hairys tend to dominate the Downys. When not dining at your feeders, Downys will continue their search for food among the trees. If you have occasion to observe them closely, you will see that the male and female Downys have different feeding strategies. The male will feed in the upper branches where the thin bark is easily drilled, while the female concentrates on the main trunks.

Downys will be readily attracted to a suet feeding station, but will also dine on fruit, peanut butter mixtures, cornbread and sunflower seeds. If you offer suet throughout the summer, you will likely have Downys carry some of it to feed their nestlings. When the young have left the nest, they will often be brought to dine at the feeder by their parents.

## HAIRY WOODPECKER
### (Picoides villosus)

Hairy Woodpeckers appear, at first glance, to be just larger, more wary versions of the Downys. They can be quite easily separated, however, as the Hairys are larger, have long bills (longer than the distance from the eye to the back of the head) and completely white outer tail feathers. Only the males have red on their napes.

Hairy Woodpeckers are attracted to suet feeders and will also eat nuts, fruit and shelled sunflower seeds. Like the Downys, they will use a summer suet feeder for both themselves and their offspring.

## PILEATED WOODPECKER
### (Dryocopus pileatus)
The Pileated is Alberta's largest and most magnificent woodpecker. Its large size and bright red cap are unmistakable. While it prefers dense, mature forests, the species seems to be adapting well to human encroachment and is becoming more common and increasingly tolerant of disturbed habitats.

Pileateds love carpenter ants, which they try to find in fallen logs or stumps or by excavating large oval holes at the base of trees. They leave behind a large pile of huge wood chips, proof of their incredible strength.

If you live adjacent to a mature mixed forest, you may be able to attract these beautiful woodpeckers to your suet feeding station. Kerry and Marjorie Wood of Red Deer have them coming to their suet feeders year round. Serve the suet on a large hanging board.

# JAYS, CROWS AND MAGPIES

Jays, crows and magpies belong to the *Corvidae* family, an extremely intelligent but raucous group that are noted for their aggressive behavior and persistence. They are omnivorous, eating seeds, scavenging carcasses or dining on the eggs and nestlings of other birds with equal ease. This group is also noted for its habit of banding together to harass or mob such potential predators as owls and hawks.

## BLUE JAY
### (Cyanocitta cristata)
Set against a background of white snow and a bright winter sky, the brilliant cobalt colors of the Blue Jay are stunningly beautiful. Armed with intelligence, an excellent memory, an insatiable curiosity and a stout bill, the Blue Jay can provide feeder watchers with hours of entertainment. The species has surprising longevity, up to 18 years, so the birds that frequent your feeder year after year may be the same individuals.

Blue Jays are common residents of northern and central Alberta, and are increasing in number in the southern part of the province, especially in Calgary.

At a feeder, Blue Jays devour corn, sunflower seeds, suet, bone sawdust and whole or shelled peanuts. They will also eat Durum wheat. When they have eaten their fill, they continue to pack off seeds or nuts in their expansible throat pouches and/or in their beaks and hide them either in the crack of a tree or by poking them in the ground.

Many feeder watchers can attest to the intelligence of these birds. Ruth Stewart of Red Deer recounts how she set out several whole peanuts one day for her Blue Jays. By shaking them, she determined that one of the peanuts contained two nutmeats while all the others contained only one. The first jay that landed at the feeder lifted up, then dropped, each peanut until it finally found the one with the two nutmeats! Joan Susut of Lacombe witnessed a Blue Jay sitting on her kitchen window ledge one morning, flapping its wings furiously against the glass. When she investigated further, she realized that the corn feeder from which it dined each morning was empty. She promptly filled the feeder and the jay left her alone!

Blue Jays may dominate a feeding station by chasing the smaller birds away. They sometimes give an alarm call when they arrive at a feeder, effectively sending the other diners scurrying for shelter. If jays continually take over your feeding station to the exclusion of other species, you might try setting out more feeding stations, using an exclusion feeder (see page 13) or serving the jays dry dog food at a station removed from the other feeders. Since jays love dry dog food, they will tend to ignore the other feeders if the dog food is readily available. Cal and Blanche Lockhart of Lac La Biche have used this segregation-feeding method successfully for several years.

It has also been suggested that Blue Jays steal other birds' eggs because they lack calcium. While it hasn't been proven, one popular theory suggests that if finely-ground eggshells are added to their food during the late winter and early spring, the jays will be less likely to rob active nests. Even if it doesn't deter them from preying on nests, the calcium is a healthy addition to their diet. See page 25 for tips on how to offer eggshells.

While most adult Blue Jays are non-migratory, first-year birds may travel south for the winter. During the late fall and early winter, Blue Jays lead a solitary existence, although several will come together at a feeding station. They will not usually tolerate other jays being too close to them at this time. Courtship starts in mid-winter, when a crowd of competing males can be seen flying about in hot pursuit of a female. They are especially vocal at this time and add two new notes (*tooltool, tooltool; wheedelee*) to their usual *jaay, jaay* call. Blue Jays also have the ability to imitate the calls of hawks, which they will often do if a hawk is in the area. This behavior has yet to be explained.

## STELLER'S JAY
*(Cyanocitta stelleri)*
The Steller's Jay is unmistakable with its conspicuous black crest, throat and upper breast. The rest of its body is a deep blue color. The Steller's Jay replaces the Blue Jay in the Rocky Mountains of Alberta, although individuals tend to wander east during the winter (they have been reported in Red Deer and Calgary). The two species have been known to hybridize.

During the winter, Steller's Jays form small groups and will often scavenge for grain amongst herds of cattle and horses. They will also frequent ground or tray feeders that are located within their winter range to eat sunflower seeds, corn and bread. Their calls include a harsh *shaack, shaack, shaack.*

## GRAY JAY
*(Perisoreus canadensis)*
This friendly rogue-of-the-woods has many aliases, including Canada Jay, Whiskey Jack, Camp Robber, Meat Hawk and Moose Bird. It is a grayish bird with a white head, black nape, short bill, long tail and no crest. A permanent resident of the heavily forested northern regions of Alberta and the Rocky Mountains and foothills, it will occasionally wander into the parkland regions of the province during the winter.

The call notes of the Gray Jay include a whistled *wheeoo* and a low *chuck.* Gray Jays are among the earliest nesters in Alberta - they are already incubating their eggs in early March.

Gray Jays are well known to back-country travellers, as they invariably appear at opportune moments, confidently expecting a handout. If none is readily offered, they will often resort to pilfering. Although Gray Jays will eat kitchen scraps, bread and shelled sunflower seeds, their favorite feeder food seems to be suet, which they will both eat and hoard. They will also eat raisins and cat food. Tom Webb of Turner Valley serves the Gray Jays at his feeder salmon-flavored cat food.

## CLARK'S NUTCRACKER
*(Nucifraga columbiana)*
The Clark's Nutcracker, sometimes confused with the Gray Jay, is a chunky gray bird with black wings and black central tail feathers. Its white wing patches and white outer tail feathers are conspicuous in flight.

Clark's Nutcrackers inhabit the subalpine coniferous forests of the Rocky Mountains. They have a loud harsh *kaar-kaar* cry.

Nutcrackers are bold birds and will readily look for a handout from tourists or hikers in the high country. In the winter, they descend to lower altitudes, appearing around towns and ski lodges where they join Gray Jays in scrounging for handouts. They will also visit ground feeders that offer sunflower seeds, suet and whole or shelled peanuts.

## BLACK-BILLED MAGPIE
*(Pica pica)*
This beautiful, successful omnivore is thought to have followed the early settlers into Alberta. Its intelligence and cunning adaptability have made it one of the most common, though not the most appreciated, birds of the settled regions of Alberta. It is an easily recognized black-and-white bird with a long, flowing tail.

Though often unjustifiably maligned, some feeder operators feel that magpies have earned their reputation through such unpopular habits as harassing other birds and eating their eggs and young, and stealing dog food right out of the dog dish (they usually do this in pairs - one diverts the dog's attention while the other one sneaks in to eat.) While they will eat kitchen scraps and sunflower seeds, their favorite feeder foods are suet and bone sawdust, which they will go to no end of trouble to acquire. Smeared or otherwise attached to tree trunks, or served in large blocks, suet and bone sawdust will inevitably be discovered by magpies. To serve both magpies and other smaller feeder species, offer some suet in feeders protected by wire mesh or by hanging out pieces too small for the magpie to land on. See page 55 for other ideas on how to magpie-proof some of your feeders.

## AMERICAN CROW

*(Corvus brachyrhynchos)*

The crow is often confused with the Common Raven. The two species are best separated in the field by their size difference (the crow is much smaller), their beak shape (the raven's beak is much heavier and longer) and their tail tip (the crow's is curved, the raven's is wedge-shaped).

The two diagrams to the right show the differences between the two species. In the top diagram, the crow is on the left. In the bottom diagram, it is on the right.

A few crows over-winter in the province each year. In the mountain towns of Blairmore, Banff and Jasper, they regularly visit feeders that offer frozen meat, kitchen scraps, suet and peanuts. They will even eat the occasional sunflower seed.

## COMMON RAVEN

*(Corvus corax)*

Ravens are year round residents in the Rocky Mountains, the foothills and the forested regions of northern Alberta. In the settled portions of central and southern Alberta, they are seen irregularly during the winter. Ravens are scavengers, often eating dead animals and garbage.

If you live in the western or northern portions of the province, you may find ravens dining at your suet feeders. They also like whole peanuts, kitchen scraps, cat food, frozen meat and, if their preferred food is in short supply, will even shell and eat sunflower seeds.

# CHICKADEES

If a popularity contest were to be held to pick our favorite winter bird, there is little doubt that chickadees would win. Like feisty little cherubs, they brighten up even the coldest and dreariest winter days with their incessant antics and chatter. According to Project FeederWatch (see page 59), they are the most common feeder species in Alberta and all of Canada.

Chickadees have a complex and fascinating social structure. During the fall, individuals forsake their breeding territory in favor of a much larger winter territory of about eight hectares (20 acres). They share this with about a dozen other adults which have bred in the area as well as young birds from other areas. Winter flocks rarely contain adults and juveniles from the same family, but some flocks consist of the same individuals year after year.

Chickadees spend the long, cold winter nights huddled together in a tree cavity or on a branch for warmth. Studies have found that their metabolic rate is slowed to the point where their body temperature is reduced from a normal range of 39°-41°C to about 30°C.

A typical winter day in the life of a flock of chickadees is spent on the ever-important quest for food, as individuals busily search the crevices of tree branches and trunks for dormant insects or other delicacies that will provide fuel for their tiny furnaces. On really cold days, you will notice that they feed and rest with their feathers fluffed out. While it may make them look a little forlorn, this practice keeps them comfortably warm as it traps an insulating layer of air next to their bodies.

Chickadees have a vocal repertoire of about 15 different calls and songs. During the winter, they use calls to keep in contact with the other members of the flock and to issue threats or warnings. In late winter and early spring they will continue to call, but also add songs to their repertoire. Songs are used to advertise territory and to attract mates.

Each chickadee flock stays within its winter territory and defends it against other flocks. If you put your suet or sunflower seed feeders out in the early fall, you will probably have little trouble convincing a flock to set up its winter territory to include your feeders. Recent research has shown that Black-capped Chickadees can remember the locations of successful feeding stations for up to eight months! If a feeder is near the territorial border of two flocks, they will both use it. When both flocks show up at the same time, you can expect territorial squabbles to ensue, with one group scolding and chasing off the other.

You will notice that chickadees usually pick one sunflower seed from the feeder and fly away with it to a nearby tree where they hold it securely in their feet and peck at it to extract the seed. If their hunger has been temporarily satiated, they will often continue carrying away seeds but, instead of eating them, will stuff them into tiny crevices, under bark or between spruce needles. This hoarding behavior is an avian insurance policy: they store up in times of plenty to ensure that there will be food around in the event of future shortages. Not surprisingly, it doesn't take long for other chickadees, nuthatches, juncos, jays and squirrels to discover these food caches.

You will be able to witness the rigid social hierarchy within the chickadee flock as it feeds, with the dominant (alpha) bird feeding first or displacing subordinate (omega) birds when they arrive at the feeder. The alpha bird is usually the male that nested near the centre of the flock's winter range while the omega birds are the juveniles. Females have their own rank order, with the juveniles also at the bottom of the heap. In times of food shortages, the juveniles will invariably starve first. This is nature's way of ensuring that adult birds, having already proven their breeding ability, are spared.

Chickadees are so tame that they can, with a little patience, be enticed to take seeds and nuts out of your hand.

There are three common species of chickadees in Alberta. A fourth, the Chestnut-backed Chickadee, has only been recorded a few times in the province.

## BLACK-CAPPED CHICKADEE
*(Parus atricapillus)*
Small gray birds with a broad, white face mask separating a black crown and throat, Black-caps are the most common of the Alberta species and are found throughout the province.

If you hear Black-caps in the winter, they are probably using one of the following calls or songs: *Chickadeedeedee* - a year round call that is usually given when there is a disturbance, when one bird becomes separated from the rest of the flock or to alert the rest of the flock that danger has passed; *Tseet* - a year round high call given between members of a flock to help them keep in touch with each other; *Tsee* - when issued sharply, means that a predator is approaching; *Fee bee bee* - a three-note whistle song given by the male during warm weather and at the onset of the breeding season, a welcome song that announces the coming spring.

Black-caps will eat suet and sunflower seeds with equal gusto. They also relish walnuts.

## MOUNTAIN CHICKADEE

*(Parus gambeli)*

The Mountain Chickadee looks like the Black-capped but is grayer and has a distinct white eye line that extends from the base of the bill to the back of the head.

Mountain Chickadees are permanent residents of the Rocky Mountain regions of Alberta, although they descend to lower altitudes and move out into the foothills during the winter. They occasionally wander farther east and have been known to show up at feeders as far east as Saskatchewan. In Alberta, they are regular visitors at feeders in our mountain towns and will show up occasionally in the central and eastern parts of the province.

Mountain Chickadees will often associate with flocks of Black-capped and Boreal Chickadees during the winter. Their call has a hoarse quality, quite unlike the other two species.

Mountain Chickadees dine on both suet and sunflower seeds. They will also eat cat food and pastry.

## CHESTNUT-BACKED CHICKADEE

*(Parus rufescens)*

This rare species can be identified by its sooty-brown cap, white cheeks, black bib and bright chestnut-colored sides, back and flanks. It has no whistled song, and its calls are hoarse and rapid.

Reinhold Lang reports having a Chestnut-backed Chickadee visit his feeder in Banff a few years ago in the late fall. It ate sunflower seeds.

If you see a Chestnut-backed Chickadee, call the Provincial Museum of Alberta in Edmonton (427-1730) or the Calgary Rare Bird Alert (237-8821).

## BOREAL CHICKADEE

*(Parus hudsonicus)*

While they look like Black-caps, Boreal Chickadees are distinctive with their brown crown, gray neck and reddish-brown flanks.

Boreals are usually absent from the prairies, but are often found in abundance where there are at least a few evergreen trees. The *chickadee* call of the boreal has been described as the call of a drunken Black-capped. They keep track of each other in their winter flocks with a wheezy *zeee-zeee*. The spring song of the male Boreal Chickadee is a clear pleasant *pit-tulululu* trill.

Boreals are reported to be aggressive at feeders, often squabbling with Black-caps and amongst themselves. They are especially fond of suet, unsalted crumbled peanuts and bran muffins. They do not usually eat sunflower seeds.

# CREEPERS

## BROWN CREEPER

*(Certhia americana)*

The Brown Creeper is an aptly-named woodland bird with a slender, down-curved bill and stiff, pointed tail feathers. It is brown in color with light streaks on its back and light buff wing bars. It has the interesting habit of flying to the base of a tree, slowly working its way upward around the trunk to the top, then moving to the next tree for a repeat performance. Creepers and nuthatches can quite easily search the same tree trunk without competing with each other for food, since nuthatches usually work from the top down while creepers work from the bottom up.

The Brown Creeper is actually quite common in the parkland and boreal forest regions of Alberta, but is so elusive that it is seldom seen and often overlooked. If you listen carefully, you may be able to hear its thin, high pitched *seeee* call. If you live in an area with lots of evergreen trees, you will likely be successful at enticing a Brown Creeper to a bone sawdust feeding station. They will also come to a hanging suet feeder, although they prefer to eat suet smeared directly on to tree trunks. See page 23 for more details on how to serve suet and bone sawdust to Brown Creepers.

# NUTHATCHES

Nuthatches have the unusual claim of being able to view the world upside down! They belong to a family of short-tailed acrobats, *Sittidae*, which spend the better part of their lives climbing down tree trunks and branches in search of food. Their name is derived from "nut-hack", a reference to the nuthatches' habit of wedging a hard-shelled nut into a bark crevice and then hammering it until it opens. They do not have a seed-crushing beak. Like the chickadees, they will hoard food by stuffing it into bark crevices.

## WHITE-BREASTED NUTHATCH
*(Sitta carolinensis)*
The White-breasted Nuthatch shuns the coniferous woods so favored by the Red-breasted Nuthatch, preferring instead mature deciduous woods that contain old trees and tall broken stumps. It, too, has a black cap, but differs from its smaller red-breasted cousin by having an all-white face and breast and brick red undertail feathers. The silver-gray or gray cap on the female is smaller than the jet black cap of the male.

White-breasted Nuthatches are quite common during the winter in the parkland regions of the province, where they can often be seen busying themselves in their never-ending search for food. A male and female maintain a loose pair bond during the winter, travelling alone but remaining within earshot of each other in their winter territories of nine to 18 hectares (25 to 50 acres). At night, each individual roosts alone in its own tree cavity.

If they find other nuthatches trespassing, a territorial dispute ensues, with the warring birds moving about on the tree trunk near each other with their heads down and their feathers ruffled. These encounters become more aggressive with the approach of the early spring breeding season. The birds then shift their attention from defending their winter range to defending a much smaller breeding territory.

White-breasted Nuthatches have an interesting repertoire of calls and songs: *Ank Ank* - given by both sexes all year to keep in contact or, if given in a series, may signify disturbance; *Ip Ip* - a higher, quiet sound issued between a pair when they are feeding close to each other; *Werwerwerwer* - the male's song, given from high in the trees in late winter or spring at the onset of courtship.

White-breasted Nuthatches will become regular visitors to feeding stations laden with nuts, sunflower seeds and suet, often feeding together at the same time. If you see a male bring a morsel of food over to the female, you can be sure that they will soon be looking for a nest cavity.

## RED-BREASTED NUTHATCH
*(Sitta canadensis)*

The smaller of the two Alberta species, the Red-breasted Nuthatch prefers to live in the vicinity of coniferous forests, where its presence may sometimes be detected only by its *nyaa nyaa nyaa* call, which is high pitched and less nasal than the call of the White-breasted Nuthatch. When seen, it is easily identified by its black cap and eye line, white eyebrows and rust underparts. Females and juveniles have duller heads and paler underparts than the males.

It has been suggested that the adult birds tend to remain in their breeding area year round while the juveniles migrate south for the winter, returning again in April, often in the company of early migrant warblers. Following a year of low cone production, it is likely that they move southward early with crossbills and other birds that depend on cone crops.

The main winter diet of the Red-breasted Nuthatch consists of spruce and other conifer seeds, but they will also dine on insects, insect eggs and larvae, and spiders. Feeders that offer chopped nuts, sunflower seeds and suet will be regularly visited by over-wintering nuthatches. Although they are usually aggressive and competitive at a feeding station, Red-breasted Nuthatches may become quite tame.

# KINGLETS

## GOLDEN-CROWNED KINGLET
*(Regulus satrapa)*

Tiny and plump, this grayish-olive bird is an inhabitant of Alberta's coniferous forests. It has a broad white eyebrow and two white wingbars. The male has an orange crown patch bordered in yellow and black, while the female's crown is yellow with black borders.

Golden-crowned Kinglets over-winter throughout the treed areas of the province, but are often overlooked because they tend to feed high in the tree crowns, sometimes in the company of chickadees, Brown Creepers and Downy Woodpeckers. They eat insects and insect eggs almost exclusively, but will occasionally come to a feeder to dine on suet.

# THRUSHES

## AMERICAN ROBIN
*(Turdus migratorius)*

Robins are both common and widespread, and seem to flourish in the presence of people. Gray-brown above, with a darker head and tail, the robin has a yellow bill and brick red underparts. The females are less intensely colored than the males.

40.

Although an over-wintering robin is still a rarity in Alberta, there seem to be a few reported every winter. Some return in the spring while temperatures are still cold and the ground covered with a thick blanket of snow.

You may be able to attract robins to your feeder by offering bread, toast crumbs, raisins, currants, fruits, berries (especially Nanking cherry and Mayday berries), raisin bread, chopped vermicelli or cooked sweet potato. They also like a mixture of peanut butter and cornmeal. Winnie Ellis of Lacombe treats the robins at her feeders to cornbread.

# WAXWINGS

## BOHEMIAN WAXWINGS
*(Bombycilla garrulus)*
## CEDAR WAXWINGS
*(Bombycilla cedrorum)*

Bohemian Waxwings nest in northern and western Alberta, then appear in southern towns and cities late in the fall to feast on the fruits of ornamental shrubs and trees. Their summer counterparts, the Cedar Waxwings, breed in north and central Alberta, then move south for the winter. A few occasionally over-winter in the province.

The Bohemians (below right) can be separated from Cedars by their cinnamon undertail coverts, gray underparts, and white and yellow wing spots. Cedar Waxwings have yellowish underparts, white undertail coverts and lack the white and yellow coloration on the wings.

If fruit and berries are scarce, waxwings will be attracted to feeders that offer raisins, currants (Australian varieties seem to be most popular), chopped fruit (including apples, pears, peaches), berries or nuts. They have also been known to eat cracked corn, wheat and bread crumbs. Aaron Collins of Lacombe even had one dine at his suet feeder one winter! Glenn and Jean McCullough of Calgary report that a flock of waxwings regularly dined in their backyard one winter on chunks of frozen banana served in half a grapefruit shell. Charlie and Winnie Ellis of Lacombe fed a flock of nearly 200 birds one winter. Their offerings of ground apples and raisins were so popular that dozens of waxwings would land on the trays of food as soon as Charlie carried them out each morning.

Some feeder operators also collect and freeze mountain ash, dogwood and other berries in the fall, then offer them to the waxwings when the natural supply runs low in late winter and early spring. Waxwings also love to bathe and drink during the winter, so will be readily attracted to a winter bird bath.

# STARLINGS

## EUROPEAN STARLING
*(Sturnus vulgaris)*
Shortly after House Sparrows were introduced to North America, European Starlings were also brought over from England and released in New York State. Like House Sparrows, starlings are aggressive cavity nesters and have successfully spread throughout the continent.

During the winter, starlings have a speckled appearance and can be distinguished in flight from other birds by their short, square tails, stocky bodies and short, triangular wings. A few over-winter in Alberta, with the majority of the population returning in early spring.

Starlings are attracted to feeders that provide suet, white millet, peanut hearts and, to a lesser extent, sunflower seeds. They will often chase other birds away. If you have trouble with starlings dominating your seed feeders, try using exclusion feeders. You can also keep them away from your suet feeders by serving the suet on the underside of a horizontal board or beneath a baffle (see page 55).

# SPARROWS

Sparrows are a widespread family of birds. Except for sharing the common characteristic of having conical bills, they are very diverse and sometimes difficult to identify. A good field guide is needed to help separate the species.

## RUFOUS-SIDED TOWHEE
*(Pipilo erythrophthalmus)*
This large ground-feeding sparrow is easily distinguished by its reddish-brown sides, red eyes, white belly and long rounded tail with large white spots. The females are brown instead of black. Juveniles lose their streaking early in the fall.

Towhees, which are most common in the coulees and river bank thickets of southern Alberta, arrive in the province at the end of April or in early May. They usually leave in late September and early October. Although furtive, they will sometimes visit ground or tray feeders, especially in the fall, that offer canary seed, shelled sunflower seeds, fine cracked corn or peanuts.

## SAVANNAH SPARROW
*(Passerculus sandwichensis)*
These common ground-feeding sparrows can be distinguished in breeding plumage by their yellow lores, streaked sides and breasts, pink feet and legs and short, notched tails.

The first Savannahs arrive in Alberta in late April. They will sometimes visit ground or tray feeders, especially those that offer cornbread. They will also eat millet and other small seeds. Most have left the province by the end of September.

## SONG SPARROW
*(Melospiza melodia)*
These medium-sized, highly variable sparrows have several subspecies. All have a broad grayish eyebrow and a broad, dark stripe bordering a whitish throat. Their underparts are whitish, with streaking on the sides and breast that often converges into a central spot. Their legs and feet are pinkish. The juveniles tend to be buffier, with finer streaking and a faintly barred tail.

Most Song Sparrows arrive back in Alberta in mid-April. They are ground-feeding birds that will sometimes visit feeders that offer white millet and sunflower seeds located near dense shrubbery or other protective cover. Most leave the province in September, but a few usually remain well into October. A few occasionally over-winter.

## AMERICAN TREE SPARROW
### (Spizella arborea)

Tree Sparrows are medium-sized sparrows with a rufous cap and a dark spot in the middle of their breast. During the winter, the rufous crown may be obscured by gray and buff edges, sometimes forming a central stripe. The upper mandible is dark-gray while the lower one is yellow.

Tree Sparrows are common spring and fall migrants through Alberta and small numbers winter irregularly as far north as the Camrose area.

Tree Sparrows are ground-feeders that prefer to stay close to a thicket or bush while they feed. They will also be attracted to a ground or tray feeder that offers blended sunflower seeds, white millet, ground wheat or buckwheat. Charis Cooper of Turner Valley, who has had Tree Sparrows over-winter in her yard for many years, serves her flock wild bird seed mix from the bowl of an old cream separator. She reports that she has seen them eating at commercial suet-seed bells. They will also eat peanut butter and suet mixtures.

## CHIPPING SPARROW
### (Spizella passerina)

Chipping Sparrows are medium-sized birds, slightly smaller than Tree Sparrows, with which they are often confused. They can be distinguished by the lack of a black breast spot, a black line through the eye and a white eyebrow line. Check a field book to confirm identification of the fall juveniles.

Chipping Sparrows are found throughout Alberta. They arrive in May, and are occasionally attracted to ground feeders that offer millet, peanut hearts or shelled sunflower seeds. They are usually seen again at feeders in September and early October, just prior to migration.

## DARK-EYED JUNCO
### (Junco hyemalis)

In late March and early April, the snow is often deep and the winds are still cold. Then suddenly, the juncos appear. Brushy roadsides, urban gardens and the edges of woodland meadows become alive with the pleasant, soft notes of these tame little ground-feeding sparrows. Although there are several subspecies of juncos in Alberta, "Slate-colored" and "Oregon" being the most common, they are easily identified. All have a dark hood, pink bill, white outer tail feathers and a dark breast sharply defined from a white abdomen. If alarmed, they flash the tail edges while issuing sharp, staccato *tschit chit chit* notes.

Juncos usually feed on the ground and will eagerly come to ground or tray feeders where millet, canola, shelled sunflower seeds, cracked grain or finely ground corn is offered. They will also search through treed areas, gleaning what the chickadees have hoarded. Feeders are especially popular with juncos after spring snowstorms.

Like chickadees, juncos have a stable social hierarchy in the winter flock, with the alpha bird dominant over all the others. Once the breeding season is in full swing, however, they break up into pairs which disperse to breeding grounds, and their diet switches to insects and fresh seeds.

In September, ground-feeding stations will be discovered again by reconvening flocks, although they may not be as important as they were in the spring because there will still be plenty of berries around for them to feed on should an early fall snowstorm hit. Juncos over-winter in Alberta each year, although never in great numbers.

## HARRIS' SPARROW
*(Zonotrichia querula)*
These large sparrows have black crowns, faces and bibs, and pink bills. Their throats are black or may show white flecks or a partial band of white. In the fall, the dark crowns have a scaly appearance and the dark brown necklaces around their white throats are very noticeable.

The Harris' Sparrow is an uncommon but regular transient in Alberta, with adults being sighted occasionally in the spring and both adults and juveniles seen in the fall. Their fall migration through the province usually begins in October, long after most of the other sparrows have headed south. Like Tree Sparrows, they like to keep close to protective shrubbery while eating. Unlike other native sparrows, however, they are very aggressive at feeders - they will even put the run on House Sparrows!

Harris' Sparrows are often reported at ground feeders in late fall and early winter. Their favorite feeder foods include shelled sunflower seeds (although they will also eat unshelled ones) and white millet. A few also over-winter, usually in the southern part of the province.

## WHITE-THROATED SPARROW
*(Zonotrichia albicollis)*
White-throated Sparrows are medium-sized brown sparrows with wide white throats bordered on the sides by well-defined dark lines, dark bills and white eyebrows that are yellow in front of the eye. Check your field book for details on juvenile plumage.

Most of the White-throats arrive back in Alberta in late April. You may be able to entice them to a tray or ground feeder by offering sunflower seeds, niger seed, chick scratch, canary seed, snowberry or Mayday berries or whole or crushed grain (especially barley). They usually leave the province by October, although Reinhold Lang of Banff, Roy Richards of Jasper and Jean McCullough of Calgary all report having individual birds remain at their feeders throughout the winter.

## WHITE-CROWNED SPARROW
*(Zonotrichia leucophrys)*
These medium-sized sparrows are similar to the White-throats but are grayer and have bold black-and-white striped crowns. Their erect posture is also distinctive. Juveniles and immature birds do not resemble the adults - check your field guide for details.

White-crowns are quite common at feeders throughout the province as they migrate to and from their breeding grounds in northern Alberta and the Rocky Mountains and foothills. Their favorite feeder foods include white millet, canary seed, corn bread and walnuts. Winnie Ellis of Lacombe offers them a special treat each spring of suet mixed with lard, peanut butter, walnuts and cornbread. Most White-crowns leave the province by mid-September, although a few occasionally over-winter.

## GOLDEN-CROWNED SPARROW
*(Zonotrichia atricapilla)*
Adult Golden-crowned Sparrows are easily distinguished by their yellow patch on a black crown. Their backs are brown and streaked while their breasts, sides and flanks are grayish-brown. Check a field guide for details on juvenile plumage.

Golden-crowns are restricted to the Rocky Mountain regions of the province and are seldom seen farther east. Kevin Van Tighem reports that they are sometimes seen in the spring in Jasper, feeding among discarded seeds on the ground under sunflower seed feeders.

## FOX SPARROW
*(Passerella iliaca)*
These large sparrows are highly variable in color and have been divided into several subspecies or races. Most races have reddish rumps and tails, reddish wings, and underparts heavily marked with triangular spots merging into a larger spot on the breast.

Fox Sparrows are furtive and wary ground feeders, but have the peculiar (and noisy!) habit of scratching among the leaves by jumping back and forth with both feet at once.

Although a few Fox Sparrows will occasionally over-winter in Alberta, most pass through the province heading south in October and November, and arrive back in mid-April. They will visit both ground and tray feeders to dine on shelled sunflower seeds and millet.

## LINCOLN'S SPARROW
*(Melospiza lincolnii)*
The Lincoln's Sparrow is a shy, short-tailed sparrow with a buffy wash, fine streaks on the breast and sides, a whitish, unstreaked belly, a gray central crown stripe bordered by reddish-brown stripes, a broad gray eyebrow and a buffy eye ring.

Lincoln's Sparrows usually arrive in Alberta in late April and may stop at feeders en route to their breeding areas around marshes, bogs and beaver ponds in the northern and western portions of the province. By the middle of September, most have left the province.

Though not a common feeder bird, the Lincoln's Sparrow will sometimes visit a feeder to feed on white millet and to search through the discarded seeds and hulls.

## SNOW BUNTINGS
*(Plectrophenax nivalis)*
Snow Buntings, often called Snowbirds, are regular and usually abundant winter visitors to Alberta. They are black-and-white birds that are tinged with rusty brown during the early winter. In the spring, this rust color wears off to reveal their brilliant black-and-white breeding plumage.

Snow Buntings remain together in flocks throughout the winter and are often seen picking up salt and gravel along roadsides. They feed on weed seeds and grain and will sometimes visit a ground feeder to dine on small seeds or blended sunflower seeds.

# BLACKBIRDS

## RED-WINGED BLACKBIRD
*(Agelaius phoeniceus)*
For many Albertans, the *konk-la-ree* call of the male Red-winged Blackbird means spring has arrived. The glossy black males are unmistakable with their red and yellow shoulder patches. Females and immatures are brown and heavily streaked.

Red-winged Blackbirds rarely over-winter in Alberta, but soon after they arrive in the spring, are often attracted to sunflower seed feeders. They will sometimes feed at them throughout the summer.

## RUSTY BLACKBIRD
*(Euphagus carolinus)*
This species is often confused with its cousin, the Brewer's Blackbird. While the Brewer's is the common blackbird of the prairies and parklands, the Rusty is a bird of more northerly areas. Their ranges overlap in the central parts of the province. The females of the two species can be differentiated by their eyes: the Brewer's have brown eyes while the Rusty's are yellow. The males are more difficult to separate, but the Rusty is an even black all over, without the strong purplish reflections on the head. The two species are most likely to be confused during spring migration.

Rusty Blackbirds often remain in Alberta into November and will occasionally over-winter at sunflower seed feeders.

# WEAVERS

## HOUSE SPARROWS
*(Passer domesticus)*
This common, aggressive member of the family *Passeridae* was introduced into North America in the mid-1800s. Adaptable, intelligent and persistent, it has spread throughout the continent. Unfortunately, the House Sparrow's aggressive nature and habit of nesting in woodpecker holes and other cavities has hastened the decline of many native cavity nesting bird species throughout North America.

The male House Sparrow is easily distinguished by his black bib while the female is a nondescript brown. She may sometimes be confused with the larger and more streaked female Purple Finch.

House Sparrows are year round residents and will be readily attracted to most feeder food, especially cracked corn, shelled sunflower seeds, white millet and bread scraps. They have just recently learned how to crack shelled sunflower seeds, so will likely take over urban feeders no matter what seeds are offered.

For some feeder operators, the cheerful chirping of House Sparrows, especially on the coldest winter day, is welcomed. For others, their aggressive domination of feeding stations frustrates all attempts at enticing native birds. Sparrows that regularly visit winter feeding stations are likely to stay into the breeding season and take over natural cavities as well as nestboxes intended for bluebirds, swallows or other native cavity nesting birds.

See page 56 for ways to reduce House Sparrow problems at your feeders.

# FINCHES

Finches are seed-eaters that belong to the family *Fringillidae*. Most fly with a characteristic undulating flight.

## PINE SISKIN
*(Carduelis pinus)*
Pine Siskins are small, sociable finches of the coniferous forests. They may, at first glance, be confused with redpolls, but lack the black chin and red crown. They have markedly streaked throats and breasts and have slightly forked tails. When they fly, they show yellow on the flight feathers and at the base of the tail.

Siskins, despite their small size, are extremely pugnacious. They provide an excellent opportunity for the feeder watcher to witness social behavior, as they squabble constantly with other birds and amongst themselves. Marie Pijeau of Sylvan Lake reports that she has even seen them attacking much larger grosbeaks by jumping on them with both feet! Marjorie and Kerry Wood of Red Deer report that siskins are often successful at driving other species away from their feeders.

Siskins are irruptive migrants - abundant some years and absent others. They usually arrive back in the province in late April or early May and stay until late October or early November. A few occasionally remain all winter.

Siskins dine on small seeds and will be readily drawn to yards that have conifers or birch trees. At feeders, they love niger and canola seed, which should be served from tube feeders. They will also dine on tray or ground feeders that offer flax and sunflower seeds. Their beaks are too small for them to open the large, striped sunflower seeds, so either serve them the small oilseed variety or grind up the large ones.

## AMERICAN GOLDFINCH
*(Carduelis tristis)*
These small, gregarious finches are often referred to as "wild canaries". The male, in breeding plumage, is a bright lemon yellow all over except for a black cap, wings and tail. The females, young and fall males are greenish with dark wings and pale yellow underparts.

Goldfinches usually arrive in Alberta in late May, just as the dandelions are going to seed, and remain until the end of September. They are readily attracted to feeders that offer niger, canola and sunflower seeds.

## CROSSBILLS

## RED CROSSBILLS
*(Loxia curvirostra)*
## WHITE-WINGED CROSSBILL
*(Loxia leucoptera)*
These bird species are aptly named, as the tips of their bills are crossed - an adaptation for removing seeds from cones. The White-winged Crossbill (shown below) is a bird of the coniferous forests and mixed-wood forests where spruce predominates. The Red Crossbill is usually found in areas dominated by pine trees.

Both crossbill species are irruptive migrants - abundant in an area one year and absent the next.

Crossbills will occasionally visit feeders to dine on sunflower seeds, niger and other small seeds. They are especially fond of extracting the seeds directly from sunflower heads.

## PINE GROSBEAK
*(Pinicola enucleator)*
Pine Grosbeaks, with their stout beaks, are well-equipped to dine on sunflower seeds. The males are crimson in color, while the females and young males are gray with a rusty orange tinge to their crowns, necks and rumps.

Pine Grosbeaks are regular winter feeder visitors in both northern and central Alberta, especially in areas with coniferous trees. Mary Reiser of Bluffton, who has fed them on her farm since 1983, reports that they usually arrive at her feeders near the end of October and stay until mid-March. She has observed that they are less aggressive at the feeders than Evening Grosbeaks. Cal Lockhart of Lac La Biche reports that they tend to frequent the feeders in his area only during extremely cold weather conditions.

Pine Grosbeaks prefer striped sunflower seeds served from ground feeders. They will also eat flax and visit tray feeders. If you live on a farm, you may also try providing additional food to the Pine Grosbeaks by setting out greenfeed bales, as they like to pick at the oat kernels.

# REDPOLLS

## COMMON REDPOLL
*(Carduelis flammea)*
## HOARY REDPOLL
*(Carduelis hornemanni)*

While these two tiny winter favorites are considered to be distinct species, they are very similar in both appearance and habit.

The Common Redpoll has a red or orange-red cap (poll) with distinct streaks on the flank, rump and under the tail. The male has a rosy breast and sides. The Hoary Redpoll is slightly larger with a smaller bill and is usually frostier and paler overall. While its poll is similar to that of the Common Redpoll, streaking on the Hoary's rump, flanks and under the tail is minimal or absent and the male's breast is usually paler and pinker. Within both species, however, there is a great deal of color variation. Common Redpolls always outnumber Hoarys in a mixed flock.

Both Hoary and Common Redpolls nest in the Arctic and sub-Arctic, then move south to spend the winter. The first flocks arrive in Alberta in mid-October, just as our other small birds are heading south. They are regular winter visitors, but their winter ranges and local abundance may vary from year to year.

Redpolls remain together all winter in flocks that can often be heard passing overhead before they are seen. They glean a variety of foods from bushes, protruding weeds, spilled grain around farm buildings and from trees, especially birch or spruce. If you are ever out walking and happen upon a snowbank covered with thousands of miniature, star-like brown scales, look up. Chances are the birch tree from which these scales were dropped will be alive with twittering redpolls busily

extracting the seeds from the tree's tassel-like cones. While feeding, redpolls have the somewhat disconcerting habit of eating for a few seconds, then scattering as if in imminent danger, only to return almost immediately to repeat the entire performance.

Redpolls can easily be enticed to ground, tray or tube feeders if niger or canola seed is offered. They will also feed on sunflower seeds (ground up seem to be the most popular), oatmeal, crushed nuts, finely cracked corn and wheat, flax and white millet. While they can open a cracked or partially broken sunflower seed, redpolls usually pick through (and scatter) the seeds opened by other feeder birds to find bits of overlooked seed meats. In extremely cold temperatures, they will also eat suet.

Murray Mackay of Ponoka rakes up the sunflower seed hulls from around his feeders each spring and stores them. The following winter, he puts them out again for the redpolls, which search eagerly through the hulls to find morsels that were previously overlooked. Mr. Mackay has also watched redpolls peel off, then eat, the skin under the outer shell of the sunflower seeds.

By the end of March, redpolls become restless and more aggressive towards each other. By mid April most have left on their way to nest in the far north.

## ROSY FINCH
*(Leucosticte arctoa)*

This is a species that contains several North American subspecies. Adults are a chocolate-brown color tinged with pink. The back of the head in most subspecies is gray and the forehead is black. They are sometimes mistakenly identified as House Sparrows.

Rosy Finches are birds of the Rocky Mountain regions of western Alberta. During the winter they retreat to lower altitudes, where they are attracted to grain, sunflower seeds and millet. Margaret Makin has fed Rosy Finches all winter at her feeders in the Crow's Nest Pass area, as has Janice Smith in Waterton. Rosy Finches have also visited feeders in Writing-On-Stone Provincial Park and are occasionally seen in Banff, Lake Louise and Jasper. Their movement into central Alberta seems to be erratic, as they are occasionally reported at feeders in the Red Deer and Innisfail areas.

In early spring, Rosy Finches begin to move back

up to their breeding grounds in the high alpine meadows. At this time, they often arrive in huge flocks at feeders in the mountain towns en route. Roy Richards of Jasper and Ruth Quinn of Banff both report that Rosy Finches arrive at their feeders by the hundreds in mid to late April and spend from one day to about two weeks devouring a seed mixture consisting of white millet, flax, milo, canary seed, ground wheat and grit.

Winter sightings of Rosy Finches in Alberta are seldom reported. If you live in the prairie or parkland areas of the province and have them coming to your feeder, contact your local nature centre or Christmas Bird Count Coordinator.

## PURPLE FINCH
*(Carpodacus purpureus)*
Purple Finches usually arrive back in Alberta during April and the beautiful raspberry-red of the male provides a welcome and striking contrast to the dull grays and browns of early spring. The female (below left) resembles a House Sparrow, but is much larger, has a much heavier beak, a deeply notched tail, a heavily streaked breast and a broad white line behind the eye. Males can sing when they are yearlings, but do not acquire their red coloration until they are two years old.

When they first arrive, Purple Finches will be readily attracted to sunflower, canola and niger seed feeders. With the onset of summer, their patronage of feeders usually decreases somewhat, as they turn their attention to berry blossoms and insects. In the fall, most feeders regain their popularity until the birds depart in late September or early October. Some Purple Finches over-winter in the province - Margaret Makin reports that a few visit her feeders in the Crow's Nest Pass irregularly throughout the winter.

There have been recent sightings in Alberta of two other finch species: the House Finch *(Carpodacus mexicanus)* and the Cassin's Finch *(Carpodacus cassinii)*. The range of both these species is expanding across North America. The female House Finch lacks the distinct ear patch of the Purple Finch while the male has a brown cap, a red or orange-red forehead, chest and rump, and brown streaks along the flanks. Its bib is clearly set off from streaked underparts. The male Purple Finch, in contrast, is raspberry-red all over the head, back, rump and breast. The Cassin's Finches has a strongly notched tail. The adult male's cap ends sharply at a brown-streaked nape, and its throat and breast are paler than the Purple Finch's, while the streaks on the side are more distinct. In both sexes, the undertail coverts are always distinctly streaked. The face pattern in the Cassin's Finch is slightly less distinct than the Purple's and the bill is a little straighter and longer. You will need a good field guide to identify these species with certainty.

Cassin's Finches sometimes over-winter at feeders located in the mountain and foothill regions of the province, including Waterton and Banff. They are attracted to feeders offering shelled or unshelled sunflower seeds. House Finches are occasionally seen in the southern and western portions of the province, usually from April through October. A few occasionally over-winter in the Crow's Nest Pass area.

In order to help document the expansion of House and Cassin's Finches in the province, call the Provincial Museum of Alberta in Edmonton (427-1730) or the Calgary Rare Bird Alert (237-8821) if you have them coming to your feeder.

## EVENING GROSBEAK
*(Coccothraustes vespertinus)*

Evening Grosbeaks are among the most popular feeder birds in Alberta. Like chickadees, they have a gregarious nature and a repertoire of pleasant calls which bring cheer to a cold winter's day.

Grosbeaks are stout birds with thick, cone-shaped, seed-crushing bills. The males are brilliant yellow, white and black, while the females are mostly silver-gray with areas of yellow on the sides, nape and neck. There is considerable variation in the black coloration of the males - some are light gray while others are deep black. Both sexes show bright white patches when they fly.

While their nesting patterns are still being documented, an increasing number of grosbeaks are remaining in the province each year to breed. Feeder operators, especially in central Alberta, regularly report fledglings at their sunflower seed feeders in mid-summer.

Large flocks of grosbeaks are found throughout most of the province (except the south-eastern portion) during the winter, especially in areas with deciduous trees. Since they remain in flocks and usually depend on tree seeds (especially Manitoba maple) for their main food source, they have to move from region to region in order to exploit local seed abundance. Thus, they may overrun your feeders one year and be completely absent the next.

While grosbeaks eat a wide variety of seeds, buds and fruits, sunflower seeds are their favorite feeder food. Sunflower seeds provide more calories, per gram, than wild seeds or insects. A recent study in Ontario found that, on average, each individual grosbeak requires about 12.3 grams of sunflower seeds per day. And, in the interest of trivia, this same study found that a grosbeak can fly between 1.76 km (1.1 mi) and 3.68 km (2.3 mi) on the energy provided by one sunflower seed!

If you are trying to attract grosbeaks to your feeder, make sure that you keep a constant, abundant supply of sunflower seeds available.

The appearance of the season's first flock is usually preceded by the arrival of a lone scout, usually a mature female. She checks out the whole area around the feeder by exploring the nearby shrubbery and trees and sampling the seeds you have offered. If all is well, chances are that the rest of the flock will arrive the next day. The same ritual is followed by a flock returning to a previously-used feeding area. The sentinel bird, which precedes the remainder of the flock by a few hours, sits atop a high tree and calls until the others arrive.

Grosbeaks seem to prefer getting their seeds from the ground or from tray feeders. It is fascinating to watch one dexterously roll a seed over and over in its bill and reverse it end for end until the seed lies along the bill's sharp edge with its peaked end pointing into the mouth. The bill then closes and shears the dry husk lengthwise. A few movements later, the unpalatable husk has been dropped to the floor and the nutmeat swallowed.

A feeder located close to a window provides an excellent opportunity to watch the grosbeaks' social behavior patterns as each bird goes through the routine of establishing or maintaining its social slot on the crowded feeder. Watch closely for the crest raise and head forward gestures. While the males tend to be dominant, females will sometimes chase off a male or refuse to be displaced by one. Grosbeaks tend to dominate smaller feeder birds, which scatter at their approach. They also have a great appetite for salt and are often attracted to salty gravel along highways or to the grit and salt that falls off the undercarriage and mudflaps of parked vehicles.

You may notice that the odd bird in your feeder flock has a white scale-like growth on its feet. This condition, called "scaly leg", is caused by a mite. The affliction doesn't seem to cause the bird discomfort, but a few individuals eventually lose parts of their feet from it. This problem is discussed in detail on page 54.

# RARITIES

Other species that are rarely reported at winter feeders in Alberta include the Common Grackle *(Quiscalus quiscula)*, Brown Thrasher *(Toxostoma rufum)*, Brown-headed Cowbird *(Molothrus ater)* and Cape May Warbler *(Dendroica tigrina)*. In some cases, these birds stay behind because they are physically handicapped or have been caught by inclement weather. In other cases, they seem perfectly healthy and the reason for them remaining at a feeder when the rest of their kind have long since departed is a mystery.

# PREDATORS, PESTS OR PROBLEMS

Pygmy Owl

House Sparrows

Red Squirrel

# PREDATORS, PESTS OR PROBLEMS

## CATS

Cats are probably the most serious of all bird predators. You can minimize cat problems around your feeders if you put a bell on your own cat and let it out only at times when the birds are not feeding heavily. If possible, encourage your neighbors to do the same. Report feral cats to a humane society or to a local pest control officer. Take preventative measures with your feeding stations by keeping them high (at least 2 m (6 to 7 ft) off the ground) and away from dense shrubbery. If problems persist, try using baffles (see page 56) or wrap a piece of galvanized metal 30 cm (1 ft) wide around the post about 1 to 2 m (3 to 7 ft) from the ground. Ground feeders, especially near shrubbery, can be protected if they are enclosed by a wire mesh fence.

## DISEASES

Contagious avian diseases can sometimes be harbored and spread at crowded feeders through contaminated droppings, mold and diseased birds. The most common cause of death among wild birds is infection by the *Salmonella* bacterium and the species that flock together in large numbers are most affected. Many infected birds remain healthy but are capable of passing on the disease, usually through infected feces. *Salmonella* causes birds to contract pneumonia when stressed by cold or hunger. Sick birds are lethargic, fluff out their feathers and may stand about with their mouths open or their heads tucked under their wings. Death follows the onset of pneumonia fairly quickly.

If you find sick or dead birds near your feeders, stop feeding immediately. Rake up the discarded seed hulls or grain and bury them away from the feeders, then scrub and disinfect all feeders. Take one or two dead birds to your nearest Alberta Fish and Wildlife office for autopsies. If possible, burn the remainder.

If you are concerned about the possibility of disease at your feeders, avoid using tray feeders since droppings can contaminate the food. Use a hopper or tube feeder that requires the birds to perch adjacent to, rather than in, the food dispenser.

To minimize the chance of infection and to combat its spread, thoroughly clean and disinfect your feeders at least once a year (more frequently if disease is present) with bleach and hot water. As an extra precaution, disinfect the perches regularly.

Feeding only during the winter months may also reduce the spread of disease.

Another common concern when birds die near feeders is whether the disease can be passed on to predators, pets or humans. During the winter of 1987, veterinarians in the north-eastern United States reported that many cats came down with "songbird fever", a condition typified by a high fever and loss of appetite that usually subsides within a week. It is suspected that the infection was caused by the cats' consumption of *Salmonella*-infected birds. For this reason, keep your cat inside until a disease outbreak is over or contained and clean your hands after changing your cat's litter box. Always wear rubber gloves when disinfecting or handling seeds from contaminated feeders and when handling dead birds.

A few individuals in most flocks of Evening Grosbeaks are afflicted with "scaly leg" (Cnemidocoptiasis). This is a condition caused by a mite (*Cnemidocoptes spp*) that tunnels into the outer skin of the bird's leg, causing an excessive growth of the outer tissues which then form into scales and crusts. The mites complete their entire life cycle on the host bird and probably continue to live and reproduce on that host until it is dead. In advanced cases, parts of the bird's feet will literally break off, making it difficult for it to walk or perch. Surprisingly, they appear to exhibit no ill-effects from this affliction other than being relegated to the bottom of the social hierarchy.

While not yet proven, some researchers suggest that transmission of the mite probably occurs most often in the nest site between adult birds and their offspring - not at feeding stations.

Other than capturing the afflicted birds and rubbing the affected areas with oil or a lindane salve, no readily available treatment is known.

## MAGPIES AND STARLINGS

These two species love suet and will go to great lengths to feed at suet stations. If you want to deter them from at least some of your feeders, the following ideas may be of some assistance.

One technique is to serve the suet in an exclusion feeder with 38 mm (1.5 in) wire (starlings can get through 50 mm (2 in) wire). Make sure the wire is placed far enough away from the suet so they can't reach through it (above right).

Dick Tuttle from Delaware, Ohio has had success detering starlings by serving suet from the bottom of a horizontal board, shown below. While the magpies and starlings cannot do so, woodpeckers, chickadees and nuthatches have little trouble feeding while hanging upside down.

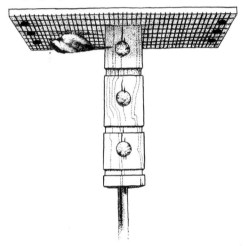

Glenn and Jean McCullough of Calgary have designed the novel and effective magpie deterrent shown below.

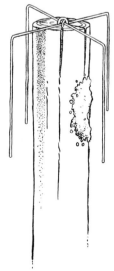

To construct this deterrent, they simply stapled straightened wire coat hangers to the top of a tall post and bent them to hang down on either side of the place where the suet is served. This prevents magpies from getting close enough to take a bite. Instead, they back off when their wings touch the wire.

Magpie traps are often effective at reducing local magpie population numbers. To obtain magpie trap plans, contact your local District Agriculturist or County Agricultural Office.

## PREDATORY BIRDS

Predation, although seemingly unpleasant, is a natural process and is important to the health of both the predator and prey species. Hawks (Goshawk, Cooper's, Sharp-shinned), Falcons (Merlin, Gyrfalcon), Owls (Great Horned, Northern Pygmy, Northern Hawk, Snowy, Boreal and Northern Saw-whet) and Shrikes (Northern) are all natural predators of Alberta's over-wintering birds and may visit a feeding area on occasion. If your feeders are close enough to protective shrubbery, the predators will probably only succeed in taking the old, sick and less alert birds.

While the presence of a hawk invariably incites its prey species to panic, owls and shrikes do not always elicit the same response. Tom Webb of Turner Valley recounts watching a shrike sing and preen while being totally ignored by the feeder birds. As soon as the singing stopped, however, the flocks scattered! He has also watched a Ruffed Grouse walk calmly by, and a nuthatch actually walk under the toes of, a roosting Great Horned Owl. When the owl started to show signs of becoming active in the late afternoon, the grouse wasn't anywhere in sight, but the chickadees, jays and nuthatches continued on with business as usual.

One predator deterrent that may work relatively well in rural areas is simply to stop feeding for a few days. The feeder birds will disperse and the predator may move on in search of easier prey.

Many feeder species will "gang up" to harass a potential predator. Termed "mobbing", this behavior often drives a predator off before it has had a chance to catch anything for dinner. If you hear a group of magpies, jays or chickadees calling excitedly, the chances are that you have a predator in your yard.

Many feeder operators enjoy seeing predatory birds, all of which are protected by law, in their yard. Some even try to attract them in by offering white mice (available at pet stores) or such delicacies as chopped beef heart.

## RACOONS AND MICE

See Squirrel section below. Seeds should be stored indoors in metal garbage cans to prevent raccoons or mice from getting at them.

## SPARROWS (HOUSE)

Urban feeders will most likely attract House Sparrows, no matter what food is served. They tend to dislike feeders that sway in the wind, though, so hanging feeders are usually less popular with them than stationary ones. You may also discourage them by withholding their favorite feeder foods (bread, cracked corn, sunflower seeds, white millet) and offering the less-preferred suet or canola. Another alternative would be to use seed dispensers with portals too small for them to get at the seeds.

To discourage House Sparrows from setting up their winter territories in your backyard, delay setting up your feeding stations until late in the fall.

You may also want to set up a live trap for sparrows in your backyard. These traps are both effective and humane, and trapped sparrows will be gratefully accepted by one of Alberta's wildlife rehabilitation centres (see page 61) where they are fed to rehabilitating hawks and owls. For the plans to build a sparrow trap, contact your District Agriculturist or write to Ellis Bird Farm.

## SPRING SNOWSTORMS

Early and mid-spring blizzards no doubt take their toll on migrating birds. Robins, Mountain Bluebirds, Dark-eyed Juncos and other native sparrows are a few of the species that arrive in Alberta early each spring and often find themselves caught in inclement spring weather.

If possible, set out grit and food immediately after a snowstorm. In addition to the regular fare of suet, ground up sunflower seeds, canola and white millet, you may try offering raisins, currants, dried or fresh apples, oranges and bananas, berries, cracked corn, bread, shelled peanuts and moist coconut. Mealworms will also be popular (to grow mealworms, see page 24).

You may also try collecting, then freezing, rose hips and mountain ash and Mayday berries during the late fall to have on hand as emergency rations after a spring storm. Marion Liles of Tulsa, Oklahoma uses a "miracle meal" ration for over-wintering insect eating birds, especially Eastern Bluebirds, in his area. He mixes cage bird pellets, raisins and berries in a base of lard or suet, then forms the mixture into small balls and sets them out as required. Perhaps this mixture could also be used here in Alberta? *Let us know if you use it!*

## SQUIRRELS

There are three squirrel species in Alberta and all will visit feeding stations. Two species, the Red Squirrel and the nocturnal Flying Squirrel, are native. Gray Squirrels (individuals of the dark phase are called Black Squirrels) were introduced into, and are now thriving in Calgary. They have since spread into Okotoks and a few other surrounding towns. While most people enjoy the presence of squirrels in their backyard, they are aggressive and may at times become a nuisance. Flying Squirrels are less of a problem because they will only visit feeding stations at night and will usually only eat their fill. They do not hoard food like the other two species.

If you try to discourage Red or Gray Squirrels, you will be amazed at their intelligence, persistence and acrobatic dexterity. It is often easier just to learn to live *with* them by serving them cracked corn at a ground feeder removed from the main feeders. Where possible, place your other feeders on steel poles 2 to 2.7 m (6 to 9 ft) high and at least 2.7 m (9 ft) away from the nearest access point from which they can leap or drop on to the feeder. Wooden support posts can usually be squirrel-proofed by slipping a sleeve of stovepipe over them. Be sure to cap the top, however, since birds sometimes fall inside.

To minimize damage by squirrels to your tube feeders, use ones made of unbreakable plastic and equipped with metal reinforced portals. Squirrels will chew through nylon rope, so suspend all feeders with wire or small chains.

Baffles are very effective at preventing squirrels from getting on to a feeder. If need be, use them both above the feeder and on the pole below it. Plastic baffles are available at most outlets that sell seed, but you can easily make your own cone-shaped ones from printing press plates (available from your local newspaper publisher) or sheet metal (see facing page). Home-made baffles can also be made out of large pop bottles or plastic salad bowls.

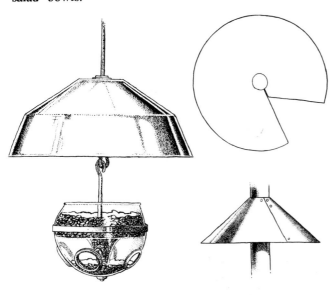

There are also commercial feeders available, called *Eliminators*, that are specifically designed to be squirrel-proof.

Glascott and Elizabeth Dawson-Grove of Calgary have designed a squirrel "zapper" that effectively deters squirrels from trying to get on to their feeders. The zapper works on the same principal as an electric fence for livestock; the squirrels receive a mild shock if they touch a "live" coil placed on the feeder pole or wire. Mr. Dawson-Grove consulted with the SPCA before using his invention, and it met with their approval.

It seems that the squirrels can actually sense the current, because, while they avoid the feeders when the unit is active, the Dawson-Groves have never witnessed one actually touching the coil. In fact, they are alerted to a malfunction of the apparatus because the squirrels resume use of the feeders as soon as the current is shut off. Once the zapper is re-connected, the squirrels immediately avoid it without ever touching it. If you would like to receive the plans for building a zapper, contact Ellis Bird Farm.

## WEASELS

Tom Webb of Turner Valley reports that weasels regularly visit his suet feeders during the winter. To date, he has seen no evidence of weasels preying upon the feeder birds. He has even watched a weasel and a nuthatch dine together on the same piece of suet (on opposite sides, of course).

## WINDOW ACCIDENTS

Casualties usually happen because birds see an expansive scene (large lawn, trees, etc.) reflected in the window, or they can see through an aligned window to the other side of the house and attempt to fly through. Window crashes also happen when the birds scatter as a predator approaches or chases them, when they chase each other, or when they see their reflections in the window and try to fight what they perceive to be a rival bird.

To minimize window accidents, move feeders that are located in front of problem windows, block reflections and put up an obstruction between two aligned windows. Other ideas include tilting the windows downward slightly ($6^0$), hanging mobiles, wind chimes or other obstructions outside problem windows, or taping the silhouette of a predatory bird on to the window. These silhouettes are available at most nature centres.

Fortunately, most birds that hit windows are just stunned. If you find one in this condition, put it in a shoe box or other cardboard box with a secure lid into which have been punched a few air holes. Leave it in a quiet, warm place for a few hours. If it revives, quietly release it near dense shrubbery.

Marjorie and Kerry Wood of Red Deer report that they have successfully treated window-crash victims for several years by following the advice given to them by a Calgary Zoo veterinarian. The vet explained that when a bird hits a window head-on, the injury usually causes blood to collect in the brain cavity. By administering a couple of drops of a half-and-half brandy/water mixture, the bird's circulation is increased and the reabsorption of blood back into its system is hastened. After administering the mixture, the Woods then set the bird carefully back outside in a protected location (shady roof-top or on a large tree branch). When the bird is recovered, it is able to leave quietly and safely.

If a bird appears to be seriously injured, contact your nearest wildlife rehabilitation centre, Alberta Fish and Wildlife Office or nature centre (see page 61).

If a bird is killed at your window, put it in a plastic bag labelled with the species name and date, and freeze it. Contact your local nature centre to see if use can be made of the accident victim.

# RESOURCE FILE

Clark's Nutcracker

Red-breasted Nuthatch (left) and White-breasted Nuthatch

# RESOURCE FILE

## KEEPING TRACK OF ALBERTA'S WINTER BIRDS

Feeder operators have made a significant contribution toward the understanding of bird behavior and winter bird population trends by documenting the activities of their feeder species. This knowledge is far from complete and important data is still being collected. If you would like to assist in this very important task, you may be interested in the following projects:

### PROJECT FEEDERWATCH

Project FeederWatch is a continent-wide feeder survey being conducted by Cornell University, New York, and the Long Point Bird Observatory in Ontario. While most of the participants in this program are from the U.S., Canadian participation is increasing every year. In order to collect accurate data, however, more Canadian participants are needed.

FeederWatchers are asked to count the birds at their feeders on one or two days every second week from November to April. Each participant pays $9 annually to support the project and in return receives four newsletters (different editions for U.S. and Canada) and a very thorough end-of-winter report. This project is an excellent way for all feeder operators to contribute to our understanding of North American feeder birds.

For more information on this project, contact Erica Dunn, Project FeederWatch, Long Point Observatory, Box 160, Port Rowan, Ontario NOE IMO.

### BIRD RECORDS

Since the Alberta Bird Record project disbanded in 1989, the collection of bird records is no longer undertaken on a provincial basis. When this book went to press, only the Calgary area had initiated a formalized, regional data collection system. All birders who live within an 80 km (50 mi) radius of Calgary are invited to submit records to this program. For more information, contact the Bird Study Group, Calgary Field

Naturalist's Society (Box 981, Calgary T2P 2K4).

For information on other regional bird record programs, contact your local nature centre or the Federation of Alberta Naturalists (Box 1472, Edmonton T5J 2N5. Phone: 453-8629).

## CHRISTMAS BIRD COUNT

Each year, thousands of bird watchers across North America spend one day during the Christmas season (December 16 through January 3) watching and counting winter birds. For some, this means tramping through the bush from dawn till dusk, while for others it means spending a half-hour walking down a back-alley. Feeder operators also participate. The Christmas Bird Count provides an excellent opportunity for beginning bird watchers to learn about our province's birds and is always a fun-filled family event.

The province is divided into count circles that are 25 km (15 mi) in diameter. Most circles have a count coordinator who oversees the logistics of the count and a count compiler who sends in the final count tally to the provincial coordinator. The results of the provincial count are carried in the journal of the Federation of Alberta Naturalists, *Alberta Naturalist*. The results from some circles are also published in the U.S. National Audubon Society's *American Birds*.

If you would like to get involved in the Christmas Bird Count, contact your nearest nature centre.

## RARE BIRD ALERT

If you see a rare or unusual bird, whether or not it is at your feeders, call either of these two numbers:

*Edmonton:* 427-1730 (Provincial Museum of Alberta - toll free via RITE line)

*Calgary:* 237-8821 (Rare Bird Hotline)

# CONSERVATION AND NATURALIST ORGANIZATIONS

The following is a list of some of the conservation and naturalist organizations in Alberta that may be of interest to feeder operators.

Alberta Environmental Network,
10511 Saskatchewan Drive,
Edmonton
T6E 4S1
Phone: 433-9302

Alberta Native Plant Council,
Box 4524, South Edmonton
T6E 5G4

Alberta Wilderness Association,
Box 6398, Station D, Calgary
T2P 2E1
Phone: 283-2025

Alberta Fish and Game
Association,
6924-104 St., Edmonton
T6H 2L7
Phone: 437-2342

Battle Lake Natural Area
Preservation Society,
c/o Box 240, Winfield
TOC 2X0

Beaverhill Bird Observatory
Society,
Box 4201, Edmonton
T6E 2T4

Bow Valley Naturalists,
Box 1693, Banff
TOL OCO

Buffalo Lake Naturalists,
Box 1414, Stettler
TOC 2LO

Calgary Field Naturalists'
Society,
Box 981, Calgary
T2P 2K4
Publish: *Pica*

Canadian Parks and Wilderness
Society,
Publish: *Borealis*
-11749 Groat Road, Edmonton
T5M 3K6
Phone: 453-8658
-Box 608, Sub PO 91
University of Calgary, Calgary
T2N IN4

Canadian Society of
Environmental Biologists (Alberta
Chapter),
c/o S. Dalton, Box 12, Sub
Station 11,
University of Alberta, Edmonton
T6G 2E0

Central Alberta Conservation
Group,
c/o D. Broadbent
RR#3, Ponoka
TOM 2H0

Edson Bird Club,
c/o Alberta Fish and Wildlife
Division,
Bag 9000, Prov. Building, Edson
TOE OPO

Edmonton Bird Club,
Box 4441, Edmonton
T6E 4T5

Edmonton Natural History Club,
Box 1582, Edmonton
T5J 2N9
Publish: *Edmonton Naturalist*

Ellis Bird Farm Ltd.,
Box 2980, Lacombe
TOC ISO
Phone: 346-2211

Federation of Alberta Naturalists,
Box 1472, Edmonton
T5J 2N5
Phone: 453-8629
Publish: *Alberta Naturalist*

Fort Saskatchewan Naturalists
Society,
c/o 10215-107 St.,
Ft. Saskatchewan
T8L 2H9

*Grande Prairie naturalists,
c/o Muskoseepi Park
9902-101 St., Grande Prairie
T8V 2P5

*Hinton naturalists,
c/o 110 Seabolt Drive, Hinton
T7V IK2

Jasper Conservation Committee,
Box 2198, Jasper
TOE IEO

Lethbridge Naturalists' Society,
Box 1691, Lethbridge
TIJ 4K4

Mountain Bluebird Trails,
c/o 1831-20th Ave. S.,
Lethbridge
TIK IG3

Red Deer River Naturalists,
Box 785, Red Deer
T4N 5H2
Publish : *Central Alberta
Naturalist*

Rocky Bird Club,
c/o Box 282, Rocky Mountain
House
TOM ITO

Sierra Club, Alberta Chapter,
621-13 Ave. S.W, Calgary
T2R OK6

Strathcona Natural History Club,
#2 Aspen View,
52250 Range Road 312,
Sherwood Park
T8G IB8

Vermilion River Natural History
Club,
Box 1769, Vermilion
TOB 4M0

Wagner Natural Area Society,
20 Forest Dr., St. Albert
T8N IX2

Wainwright Wildlife Conservation
Society,
c/o Box 1770, Wainwright
TOB 4PO
Phone: 842-5513

* informal group

# WILDLIFE REHABILITATION CENTRES

## NORTHERN ALBERTA

The Alberta Society for Injured
Birds of Prey
c/o Karl Grantmyre
51562 Range Road 222,
Sherwood Park
T8C 1H4
Phone: 922-3024

Cathie Monson
13932-109 Ave., Edmonton
Phone: 455-6471

Alberta Bird Rescue Association
c/o David and Kim Allan
51080 Range Road 223,
Sherwood Park
T8C IG9
Phone: 922-6103

## CENTRAL ALBERTA

Medicine River Wildlife
Rehabilitation Centre
c/o Carol Kelly
Box 115, Spruce View
TOM IVO
Phone: 728-3467

## SOUTHERN ALBERTA

Calgary Zoo
Box 3036, Station B, Calgary
T2M 4R8
Phone: 265-9310

Alberta Birds of Prey
Conservation Centre
c/o Colin Weir/ Wendy Slator
Box 1494, Coaldale
TOK OLO
Phone: 435-4262

# NATURE CENTRES

## CALGARY

Inglewood Bird Sanctuary
c/o City of Calgary, Parks and
Recreation Department, Box
2100, Station M, Calgary
T2P 2M5
Phone: 269-6688

Shannon Terrace Environmental
Education Centre
Fish Creek Provincial Park
Box 2780, Calgary
T2P OY8
Phone: 297-7827

## EDMONTON AREA

John Janzen Nature Centre
Box 2359, Edmonton
T5J 2R7
Phone: 434-7446

Strathcona Wilderness Centre
c/o Recreation, Parks and
Culture Dept.
County of Strathcona,
2025 Oak St., Sherwood Park
T8A OW9

## GRANDE PRAIRIE

Muskoseepi Park Pavilion
c/o City of Grande Prairie,
9902-101 St., Grande Prairie
T8V 2P5
Phone: 538-0451

## LETHBRIDGE

Helen Schuler Coulee Centre
910-4 Ave. S, Lethbridge
TIJ OP6
Phone: 320-3064

## LLOYDMINSTER

Bud Miller All Seasons Park
Centre
c/o City of Lloydminster,
5011-49 Ave., Lloydminster,
Sask.
S9V OY8
Phone: 875-4497

## MEDICINE HAT

Police Point Interpretive Centre
c/o Parks Department,
580-1 St. SE, Medicine Hat
TIA 8E6
Phone: 529-6225

## TOFIELD

Beaverhill Lake Nature Centre
Box 30, Tofield
TOB 4JO
Ph: 662-3191

## RED DEER

Kerry Wood Nature Centre
#1-6300-45 Ave., Red Deer
T4N 5H2
Phone: 346-2010

# ALBERTA FISH AND WILDLIFE OFFICES

Most Alberta Fish and Wildlife offices can be contacted free-of-charge during business hours through the RITE system.  Consult your AGT directory under "Government of Alberta" for local RITE numbers.

| | | | |
|---|---|---|---|
| Athabasca | | | 675-2419 |
| Barrhead | 674-8236 | RITE: | 134-1236 |
| Blairmore | 562-7331 | RITE: | 182-1231 |
| Bonnyville | | | 826-3142 |
| Brooks | 362-5551 | RITE: | 166-1232 |
| Calgary | 297-6423 | RITE: | 161-6423 |
| Camrose | 679-1225 | RITE: | 143-1225 |
| Canmore | | | 678-2373 |
| Cardston | 653-4331 | RITE: | 186-3159 |
| Claresholm | 625-3301 | RITE: | 168-1450 |
| Cochrane | | | 932-2388 |
| Cold Lake | | | 639-3377 |
| Coronation | | | 578-3223 |
| Drayton Valley | | | 542-6767 |
| Drumheller | 823-5740 | RITE: | 164-1214 |
| Edmonton | 427-3574 | RITE: | 427-3574 |
| Edson | 723-8244 | RITE: | 130-1011 |
| Evansburg | | | 727-3635 |
| Fairview | | | 835-2737 |
| Foremost | | | 867-3826 |
| Ft. Chipewyan | | | 697-3636 |
| Ft. McMurray | 743-7200 | RITE: | 136-7200 |
| Ft. Vermilion | | | 927-4488 |
| Fox Creek | | | 622-3421 |
| Grande Cache | | | 827-3356 |
| Grande Prairie | 538-5265 | RITE: | 121-5265 |
| Hanna | 854-5540 | RITE: | 165-5540 |
| High Level | | | 926-2283 |
| High Prairie | 523-6520 | RITE: | 122-6520 |
| High River | 652-7170 | RITE: | 177-8320 |
| Hinton | 865-8264 | RITE: | 132-8264 |
| Kananaskis | | | 591-7222 |
| Lac La Biche | 623-5247 | RITE: | 137-1247 |
| Leduc | | | 986-6775 |
| Lethbridge | 381-5266 | RITE: | 181-5266 |
| Lloydminster | 871-6495 | RITE: | 145-6495 |
| Manning | | | 836-3065 |
| Medicine Hat | 529-3680 | RITE: | 184-3680 |
| Nordegg | | | 721-3949 |
| Olds | 556-4215 | RITE: | 154-1215 |
| Oyen | | | 664-3614 |
| Peace River | 624-6439 | RITE: | 120-6439 |
| Pincher Creek | 627-3366 | RITE: | 188-1141 |
| Ponoka | 783-7093 | RITE: | 159-7093 |
| Provost | | | 753-2433 |
| Red Deer | 340-5142 | RITE: | 151-5142 |
| Rocky Mtn. House | 845-8230 | RITE: | 150-8230 |
| St. Paul | 645-6313 | RITE: | 139-1313 |
| Slave Lake | 849-7110 | RITE: | 135-7110 |
| Smokey Lake | | | 656-3556 |
| Spirit River | | | 864-4101 |
| Stettler | 742-7510 | RITE: | 153-7510 |
| Stoney Plain | | | 963-6131 |
| Strathmore | | | 934-3422 |
| Swan Hills | | | 333-2229 |
| Valleyview | | | 524-3605 |
| Vegreville | 632-5410 | RITE: | 140-1410 |
| Vermilion | 853-8137 | RITE: | 141-1137 |
| Vulcan | | | 485-6971 |
| Wetaskiwin | 352-1250 | RITE: | 144-1250 |
| Whitecourt | 778-7112 | RITE: | 148-7112 |

# RECOMMENDED READING

## FIELD GUIDES

*The Audubon Society Master Guide to Birding.* 1983. John Farrand, Jr., ed. Alfred A. Knopf, Inc., New York.

*Comments*: an advanced field handbook with excellent photographs; contains three volumes.

*Birds of North America: A Guide to Field Identification.* 1983. Chandler Robbins. Golden Press, New York.

*Comments*: excellent starter field guide; small size makes it easy to carry in the field; illustrations are small; slightly out-of-date.

*A Field Guide to the Birds of North America.* 1987. S.L. Scott. National Geographic Society, Washington, D.C.

*Comments*: most up-to-date, with most up-to-date name changes; illustrations are larger and more detailed than the other field guides; shows plumage and subspecific variations; larger and heavier than the other guides; the most expensive.

*A Field Guide to the Birds of Western North America.* 1980. Roger Tory Peterson, ed. Houghton Mifflin Co., Boston.

*Comments*: small size makes it easy to carry in field; pointers highlight identifying features; illustrations often separated from written sections; slightly out-of-date.

# BEHAVIOR WATCHING

*A Guide to Bird Behavior, Volumes 1 and 2.* 1979 and 1983. Donald and Lillian Stokes. Little, Brown and Co., Boston.

*Comments*: these fascinating books open up a whole new world of bird behavior watching. Volume 1 has more winter birds found in Alberta than Volume 2.

# ATTRACTING BIRDS

*The Audubon Society Guide to Attracting Birds.* 1985. Stephen W. Kress. Charles Scribner's Sons, New York.

*Comments*: thoroughly covers all aspects of attracting birds; does not include species descriptions; most of the plantings listed are not hardy in Alberta.

*Attracting Backyard Wildlife.* 1989. Bill Merilees. Whitecap Books, Vancouver.

*Comments*: black-and-white photographs and line drawings; covers a variety of wildlife (including frogs and snakes) with unique ideas on how to attract them; written for British Columbia, so many plant and animal species listed are not relevant to Alberta.

*The Backyard Bird Watcher.* 1979. George H. Harrison. Simon and Schuster, New York.

*Comments*: black-and-white and color photographs; covers all aspects of backyard bird watching, including photography and binoculars.

*Backyards For Wildlife: Spring and Summer Season.* 1987. Myrna Pearman. Red Deer River Naturalists and Kerry Wood Nature Centre, Red Deer.

*Comments*: line drawings; provides a summary of techniques for setting up a backyard for wildlife; provides a list of Alberta-hardy plantings useful to birds and other wildlife; available at $5 per copy (plus $1 for shipping and handling) from the Red Deer River Naturalists Box 785, Red Deer, Alberta T4N 5H2.

*The Birds Around Us.* 1986. Alice E. Mace, Ed. Ortho Books, San Fransisco.

*Comments*: color photographs and line drawings; very comprehensive and includes other information about bird behavior, natural history and so on.

*The Bird Feeder Book: An Easy Guide to Attracting, Identifying, and Understanding Your Feeder Birds.* 1987. Donald and Lillian Stokes. Little, Brown and Co., Boston.

*Comments*: good summary; excellent photographs; many of the feeder species discussed are not found in Alberta.

*Feeding Wild Birds in Winter.* 1981. Clive Dobson. Firefly Books Ltd., Scarborough, Ontario.

*Comments*: line drawings; species descriptions are very brief.

*Garden Birds - How To Attract Birds To Your Garden.* 1985. Noble Proctor. Quarto Publishing, London.

*Comments*: color photographs and color illustrations; covers all aspects of setting up a backyard for birds.

*A Garden of Birds.* 1988. Andre Dion. Quebec Agenda Inc.

*Comments*: color photographs; very comprehensive summary of how to attract birds to a backyard through plantings; many of the plantings listed are not hardy in Alberta.

*How to Attract Birds.* 1983. Jessie Wood, Ed. Ortho Books, San Francisco.

*Comments*: color photographs and line drawings; information from this book is included in a similar publication, *The Birds Around Us* (see previous listing).

*How to Attract, House and Feed Birds.* 1974. Walter E. Schultz. Collier Macmillan, New York.

*Comments*: black-and-white photographs; out-of-date but has several useful suggestions.

*Landscaping For Wildlife.* 1987. Minnesota Department of Natural Resources, St. Paul.

*Comments*: line drawings, color illustrations and color photographs; probably the most comprehensive publication on this topic; contains information pertinent to both urban and rural landowners; very exhaustive appendices covering plantings, feeder designs, plant diseases and so on.

*A Time For Fun.* 1967. Kerry Wood. Kerry Wood, Red Deer.

*Comments*: line drawings; includes one chapter on winter bird feeding in Alberta.

# GENERAL

*The Audubon Society Encyclopedia of North American Birds.* 1980. John K. Terres. Alfred A. Knopf, New York.

*Comments*: an A to Z of North American birds; superb photographs.

*The Birds of Alberta*. 1976. R.W. Salt and J.R. Salt. Hurtig Publishers, Edmonton.

*Comments*: was intended to supplement, not replace, a field guide; contains very interesting life-history information on each species; some sections are out-of-date (especially range maps).

*The Birds of Canada*. 1986 (revised edition). W. E. Godfrey. National Museums of Canada, Ottawa.

*Comments*: large, coffee-table size; contains the most accurate range maps for Canada; illustrations separated from text.

*The Nature of Birds*. 1988. Adrian Forsyth. Camden House Publishing, Camden East, Ontario.

*Comments*: superb photographs; covers the general life-history of birds.

*The Wonder of Canadian Birds*. 1985. Candace Savage. Western Producer Prairie Books, Saskatoon.

*Comments*: well written with lots of superb photographs; gives natural history information on selected species.

# PERIODICALS

*Birder's World*
-published bi-monthly
-standard magazine format
-very high quality stories and photographs covering all aspects of interest to amateur and professional ornithologists
-Address: Subscription Department, Box 1347, Elmhurst, Ill. 60126-8347

*Bird Watcher's Digest*
-published bi-monthly
-small book format
-emphasis is on U.S. birds, but lots of useful tips on winter bird feeding, wildlife gardening, identification, etc.
-Address: Box 110, Marietta, Ohio 45750

*Living Bird Quarterly*
-published quarterly
-standard magazine format
-high quality magazine that deals with all topics of interest to both professional ornithologists and amateur birders
-Address: Cornell Laboratory of Ornithology, 159 Sapsucker Woods Road, Ithaca, New York 14850

*Nature Society News*
-published monthly
-newspaper format
-deals mostly with Purple Martins but does carry articles on bird feeding during the winter months
-Address: Purple Martin Junction, Griggsville, Ill. 62340

# WE'D LIKE TO HEAR FROM YOU!

If you have any comments, ideas or observations that you would like to share with other feeder operators, or would like to see included in a revised edition of this book, we'd be happy to hear from you. We are especially interested in finding out about innovative bird feeder designs and would appreciate getting feedback about sunflower seed type preferences, the use of "miracle meal" emergency ration (described on page 57) and the use of Sharp-tailed Grouse feeding stations (described on page 31). We are also interested in sightings and behavioral observations of less-common species.

Please send all comments or queries to: Myrna Pearman, Biologist, Ellis Bird Farm Ltd., Box 2980, Lacombe, Alberta. TOC ISO. Phone (403) 346-2211.